Human Resource Management

Dedicated to Val, Orla, Lily, Phoebe, Jake and Nathan

SAGE COURSE COMPANIONS

KNOWLEDGE AND SKILLS for SUCCESS

Human Resource Management

John Martin

Los Angeles • London • New Delhi • Singapore • Washington DC

First published 2009

Apart from any fair dealing for the purposes of research
or private study, or criticism or review, as permitted
under the Copyright, Designs and Patents Act, 1988, this
publication may be reproduced, stored or transmitted in
any form, or by any means, only with the prior
permission in writing of the publishers, or in the case of
reprographic reproduction, in accordance with the terms
of licences issued by the Copyright Licensing Agency.
Enquiries concerning reproduction outside those terms
should be sent to the publishers.

SAGE Publications Ltd
1 Oliver's Yard
55 City Road
London EC1Y 1SP

SAGE Publications Inc.
2455 Teller Road
Thousand Oaks, California 91320

SAGE Publications India Pvt Ltd
B 1/I 1 Mohan Cooperative Industrial Area
Mathura Road
New Delhi 110 044

SAGE Publications Asia-Pacific Pte Ltd
33 Pekin Street #02-01
Far East Square
Singapore 048763

Library of Congress Control Number: 2007933697

British Library Cataloguing in Publication data

A catalogue record for this book is available from
the British Library

ISBN 978-1-4129-4509-7
ISBN 978-1-4129-4510-3 (pbk)

Typeset by C&M Digitals (P) Ltd., Chennai, India
Printed in India by Replika Press Pvt. Ltd
Printed on paper from sustainable resources

contents

Part One   Introducing your companion   1

Part Two   Core areas of the curriculum   11

2.1 Managing people in a social context   13
2.2 Human resource management and organisations   18
2.3 The legal context, including contracts of employment   26
2.4 HR planning, resourcing and retention   36
2.5 Training and development   46
2.6 Performance management   56
2.7 Remuneration and benefit management   66
2.8 Employee relations and representation   78
2.9 Discipline and grievance handling   90
2.10 Equality and diversity   100
2.11 Health, safety and welfare   110
2.12 Strategy and HRM   121
2.13 International HRM   131

Part Three Study, writing and revision skills
            (in collaboration with David McIllroy)   143

3.1 How to get the most out of your lectures   144
3.2 How to make the most of seminars   147
3.3 Essay writing tips   150
3.4 Revision hints and tips   156
3.5 Exam tips   163
3.6 Tips on interpreting essay and exam questions   169

Glossary   174
Bibliography   195
Useful websites   198
Index   200

part one

introducing your companion

This SAGE Course Companion offers you an insider's guide into how to make the most of your studies and grasp the key concepts covered in your human resource management (HRM) course. It will provide you with essential help to enhance your understanding of **HRM** and develop your thinking skills in line with course requirements. It will also help you with revision for your exams, and in preparing and writing assignments.

This book should be used as a supplement to your HRM textbook and lecture notes. You may want to glance through it quickly, reading it in parallel with your course syllabus, noting where each topic is covered in both. Ideally, you should buy this book at the beginning of your HRM course – it will provide you with a quick explanation of any topics you are having trouble with, and of course the advice on getting the most from your course will not be much help if you have already finished!

It isn't intended to replace your textbooks or lectures – it is intended to save you time when you are revising for your exams or preparing coursework. Note that revision implies that you are refreshing your memory and focussing your understanding of previously studied material in preparation for an assignment and/or exam!

This Companion will help you to anticipate exam questions, and gives guidance on what your examiners will be looking for. It should be seen as a framework within which to organise the subject matter, and to extract the most important points from your textbooks, lecture notes, and other learning materials from your HRM course.

This book should direct you to the key issues in the HRM field. Whichever textbook you are using, the basics are the basics and we have given some guidance on where topics are covered in specific books. However, you should read the Companion in parallel with your textbook to identify where specific topics are covered in it because some topics appear in more than one location in a textbook. For example, performance appraisal has relevance to reward management, training and career development and might be covered in each of those chapters in a textbook.

There is also a study and revision skills guide in Part Three which will help you to learn more efficiently. Learning is best accomplished by studying a topic from several different angles – which is why you are strongly encouraged to attend lectures and tutorials; read the textbook; and read around the subject in general. This book will help you to bring together these different sources.

How to use this book

Ideally, you should have bought this book before your course starts, so that you can get a quick overview of each topic before you go into the lecture – but if you didn't do this, all is not lost. The Companion will still be equally helpful as a revision guide, and as a way of directing you to the key themes and topics in HRM.

This first part introduces your Companion and also provides some insight on how to think like an HRM practitioner; it will help you to get into the mindset of the subject and think about it critically. As a bonus, it also means learning how to think like your examiner! Examiners want to see that you can handle the basic concepts of the subject appropriately; if you need a quick overview of the background to HRM, this is the section you will find most useful.

Part Two goes into the curriculum in more detail, taking each topic and providing you with the key themes and debates. Again, this does not substitute for the deeper coverage in your lectures and textbook, but it does provide a 'primer' to use before lectures or as subsequent revision guide – or, of course, both. Each section in this part contains the following features:

- Material presented in summary form and tips on handling the information in assessed work that also serve as reminders of key issues. These will help you to anticipate assessment questions and to remember the main points when answering them.
- 'Think about it?' boxes. These serve several purposes, for example: putting the theory into a 'real-world' context; asking you to undertake further research or reading; or prompting you to think about and draw reasoned conclusions about a particular issue. All of these can be used to strengthen your understanding of a topic and used in exams and/or coursework to elaborate and

deepen the points you make. This reflects the type of thinking that moves you from a bare pass level of answer towards a 2:1 or a First!

- Input from key thinkers in the HRM field. These will be useful to quote in exams, as well as providing you with the main influences in the development of HRM.

- Sample exam and assignment questions with outline answers. These should help you be better prepared for the actual questions, even though they will (of course) be different.

- Textbook guides. These will direct you to the main chapters from major text-books that build on what has been covered in each section in Part Two of your Companion.

Part Three of this Companion is a study guide which will help you in getting more from your lectures, remembering more when you are sitting exams, and with writing essays.

The final section of this Companion is a handy compendium of useful information, including a glossary, bibliography, list of useful websites and a general index of key terms.

Thinking like a well-informed HRM student

HRM is a relatively young discipline, and it is important to note that there is still considerable disagreement and debate among academics and practitioners about what HRM is and what it is not.

The difficulty in seeking to define HRM arises because the term 'human resource management' is used in two different ways. Firstly it can refer to the department within an organisation that has the responsibility for policy and practice in relation to 'people management' within the business. The primary activities embraced within such a department would typically be those covered by most HRM textbooks, including this Course Companion. As such it reflects a discrete subset of the management activities within the organisation and can be differentiated from the marketing, finance, production, design and engineering departments. Used in the second way, HRM seeks to reflect a particular approach to the management of people as distinct from the earlier approach adopted under the umbrella term 'personnel management'. Because the practices associated with the organisational need to manage people are subject to constant adaptation as a consequence of fashion, legislative, social, educational, organisational, economic and **labour market** changes it has been argued that personnel management had become outdated and that the philosophy, focus and approach to people management offered by HRM more effectively met the needs of modern organisations.

It is useful to reflect on the origins of HRM in order to better understand it and the current debate about its definition. The management of people has existed for many thousands of years in one form or another. Consider for example the Roman Empire and the need to 'run it', with all that this implies. The military, political and trading activities all needed people to run them and, while much of the labour was slavery based, people still needed to be directed, controlled and organised in order to meet the needs of 'empire'. In modern organisations staff must be recruited, persuaded to stay, trained, motivated, paid, directed, and so on – all within the cultural and legal conventions of the time and location. In that sense HRM simply reflects the latest in a long line of people-management approaches. The major difference today compared with the past is that people management has become a discrete and specialised discipline within management as opposed to being part of every manager's job. To some extent things have turned full circle in that it is now increasingly recognised that the management of people is a major line management responsibility and that the function of HR is to facilitate that responsibility, not to subvert it by taking responsibility away from the line manager.

Modern HRM began to emerge in the nineteenth century, based on the work of social reformers such as Robert Owen. The Industrial Revolution had fuelled the growth in factories and large urban development and as a result had changed the way that work was organised. Working and living conditions were poor and this led to demands for fundamental social reform. This pressure for change continued into the early years of the twentieth century. Torrington et al. (2005) identify five phases of personnel and HR management over that period. They are:

1 *Social justice.* Covering the period just described, this phase saw the beginnings of personnel management in the search to reduce the exploitation of workers and to be able to offer welfare services. It was the influence of major business owners such as Rowntree and Cadbury who, based on their Quaker beliefs, encouraged the development of a caring employer approach during this period.

2 *Humane bureaucracy.* This phase saw the development of a greater involvement in a range of people management activities for the fledgling personnel specialists. In the UK, for example, during the First World War vast numbers of men were taken away from their usual work and conscripted into the armed forces. They were largely replaced by women who undertook those roles for the first time. Staffing and training issues came to the fore and of course, given the

nature of war, welfare retained its significance. Following this great upheaval the **human relations movement** emerged (which emphasised social relations in the workplace) as a counter trend to the previous scientific management emphasis.

Think about it?

What welfare and other people management issues might have become significant during the First and Second World Wars? Why?

---

3 *Negotiated consent.* Following the Second World War (the late 1940s onwards) labour became a scarce commodity due to relatively high employment levels. This contributed to a growth in the membership and bargaining power of the trade unions. As a result managers needed to find ways of managing the conflict and working within a collective bargaining framework. The need for personnel officers to work in these areas was identified and encouraged by the governments of the time. Government assistance with advice and conflict resolution was provided through a body that was eventually to become the Advisory, Conciliation and Arbitration Service (**ACAS**).

4 *Organisation.* By the late 1960s personnel specialists began to take responsibility for developing training and career planning activities within organisations in addition to the above responsibilities. This period saw the emergence of a management orientation (in addition to a worker focus) to the work of personnel practitioners.

5 *Human resource management.* This emerged during the late 1980s. Given the previous discussion about the difficulty in defining HRM it is not surprising that there exists a range of perspectives on the differences between HRM and personnel management. It has been argued by some that personnel management reflected a management function that sought to represent the management to the workers and the workers to management. On the other hand HRM has been described as the management discipline that sought to ensure the **recruitment**, training, **motivation** and management of employees in a way that maximised their utility to management. In that sense totally management focussed and supportive.

If you take nothing else away from this discussion be aware that many social, cultural, organisational and legal factors have changed over the years and that personnel management has evolved into the present day HRM within that changing environment.

The above discussion refers to the evolution of HRM over the past 150 years or so. In academic terms the question of what differentiates personnel management and HRM is comprehensively addressed by Legge (2005). Professor Legge identifies four types of personnel management model, including:

1 *Normative models.* Models that broadly define it as, 'the optimum utilisation of human resources in pursuit of organisational goals.'

2 *Descriptive-functional models.* Models that broadly define it as the regulation of employment relationships.

3 *Critical-evaluative models.* Models that broadly define it as being 'concerned with assisting those who run work organisations to meet their purposes through the obtaining of the work efforts of human beings, the exploitation of those efforts and the dispensing with of those efforts when they are no longer required. Concern may be shown with human welfare, justice or satisfaction but only insofar as this is necessary for controlling interests to be met and, then, always at least cost.' based on Watson (1986).

4 *Descriptive-behavioural models.* Models that seek to describe what it is that personnel specialists actually do in the course of their work.

You may well be asked to compare and contrast the differences between personnel management and HRM. Remember that no single view is totally correct – you are expected to evaluate them all in reaching a reasoned conclusion!

Legge then develops a critical discussion on what HRM might be and how it might differ from personnel management, in the process drawing distinctions between definitions created in the USA and those from British academics (2005: 102–5). The main distinction offered is grounded in the view that HRM is intended to be more closely and tightly integrated with business strategy and **objectives**, offering a means through which the management of an organisation can more effectively 'make use' of and ensure the maximum contribution from the labour resource. Legge goes on to recognise that there are variations on this simplistic differentiation through the introduction of a 'hard' and a 'soft' view of what HRM is about. The hard version reflects the view of HRM already outlined; effectively, an asset to be manipulated by management in pursuit of operational objectives and not dissimilar in practice to any other resource. The soft version of it regards the status of employees as 'valued assets, a source of competitive advantage through their commitment, adaptability and high quality (of skills, performance etc).' (2005: 105). In essence it regards the human resource as a less passive, more responsive and interacting resource than the approach adopted by the hard view of HRM.

Storey (1992) creates a second variable to the 'hard–soft' differentiation of HRM approaches. He adds a 'strong–weak' dimension, with strong representing what could be described as the adoption of HRM as a distinct approach to labour management; and weak representing the adoption of HRM as no more than a replacement term for personnel management practice. The following factors are have impacted on the 'reformulation' of personnel management into HRM during the 1980s:

- Market changes: a marked increase in globalisation of markets and the intensification of competition. This, and some of the other changes identified below, also had a major impact on the ability of the **trade unions** to effectively represent employees and prevent or limit management intentions with regard to downsizing or relocating jobs to areas of cheaper labour.
- Technological changes: the growth and development in IT-based manufacturing and communication technologies.
- Economic changes: there was an economic downturn in the 1980s which led to the loss of skilled jobs in traditional industries and the creation of new jobs (usually lower paid and lower skilled) in new industries.
- The Japanese effect: the rapid growth of the so-called 'Japanese miracle' resulted in a focus on the associated labour management practices. Many attempts were made to 'westernise' aspects of Japanese management practice, including their approach to people management.
- Political changes: there were political changes as a result of the Thatcher and Regan eras in the UK and USA. Both governments moved to the political right with the associated political, business, enterprise, free-trade, individualism and economic effects that resulted – all of which had an impact on how people related to work and how they were managed.

Although HRM is often thought of as a discrete management discipline, it subdivides into a number of very different specialisms. Each has some degree of commonality but there is also a high degree of difference between them. There are two ways in which the work of HR specialists differs. First, it differs in the level of the postholder; for example, there are trainee, generalist, specialist, senior specialist, manager and director levels of job within the function. Secondly, there are the various subdisciplines within the HRM profession. Remember that although there is a degree of commonality between the different disciplines within

HRM, there will inevitably also be conflicting points of view and perspectives. For example, a reward specialist might recommend the introduction of **performance management** linked directly to the salary review of each employee as the best way to maximise performance; the **employee relations** and **employee development** specialists might argue very strongly that it would be counterproductive. They may argue that employee morale might be eroded by such a scheme; that performance is difficult to define for many jobs; that achieving consistency in performance evaluation across managers is difficult (if not impossible); and that higher levels of performance and commitment can be achieved through other HR initiatives such as improved **work-life balance** and development programmes. There is no one best theory or model for any HR activity, each option has a mixture of positive and negative benefits and people from a range of disciplines within HRM who will support (sometimes fiercely) each point of view. Thinking like an HR practitioner requires an understanding of the context within which HR must operate, and being able to understand the relative arguments for and against the variations in HR practice available.

To summarise the original purpose of this section – how can you think like an HR practitioner? Here are some suggestions:

- Understand the evolution of people management practice.
- Understand what HRM means to you.
- Understand what HRM means to your employing organisation – or if you are a full-time student without an employer, what might it mean to a company that you have worked for in a part-time or vacation capacity, or to one that you might like to work for in the future. Also, what does it mean to your lecturer?
- Understand what HRM might mean to colleagues and employees (if you are employed) or fellow students if you are a student.
- Understand that there are many different views on what HRM is about and that there is no single view that would be universally accepted by all **stakeholders** or academics.
- Understand the sub-disciplines within HRM and how they can contribute to the effective management of people.
- Adopt a 'critical' perspective on all aspects of HRM theory and practice. There is no perfect model, theory or understanding of human behaviour and so every idea that you encounter can be criticised – get used to uncertainty and regard it as a strength in understanding how to effectively manage people at work.
- Monitor the news media, professional and academic literature and magazines – the models, theories, case studies, examples and ideas contained in them can be used as a means of strengthening your understanding of HRM.

- Try to speak to HR practitioners in order to get their views and experiences in relation to HRM theory and practice.
- Similarly try to speak to employees and managers (perhaps among family and friends) who work in organisations where they have an HRM department to seek out their views about it.
- Think about how you would deal with the people management issues that you come across in the press, from people that you talk to, case studies and professional and academic literature.
- Participate in tutorial and other discussions about HR topics and issues with fellow students and lecturers.

Taking it **FURTHER**

You may be asked to critique theory (other words used that carry a similar connotation include critically evaluate, compare, contrast, justify and discuss) and even if you are not it is no bad thing to do so anyway. At undergraduate level, you are not required to show criticality in great depth, but you should reflect on the relative strengths and weaknesses of particular ideas or theories and also critically evaluate competing theories or models. To be able to do so will attract much higher marks than simply describing what is already known about the topic in question. Describing ideas that already exist does not demonstrate the intellectual development that is the fundamental purpose of an undergraduate degree. If you are studying at Masters level you will be required to offer a depth of critical evaluation of the ideas that you are working with so in order to produce work of Masters degree quality.

Criticality means that you have thought about the theories you are being presented with, not merely remembered them. If you disagree with a theory, and can argue the case well enough, it will be to your credit – as long as you really understood the theory in the first place! Throughout this guide there will be points at which the theory will be critiqued: obviously you will form your own ideas, and you should not be afraid to use them, but the 'Think about it' boxes are intended to begin to develop your ability to critique theory and practice in relation to HRM.

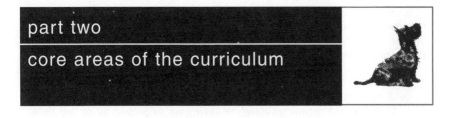

Underlying themes in human resource management

As with any management or business discipline there are a number of underlying themes that would be relevant to any course in human resource management. These are identified below and each is developed further in the detailed discussion in subsequent sections of this part of the Course Companion. Each of these significant themes also forms part of the understanding of human resource management that you would be expected to demonstrate when answering assignment or examination questions. The themes include:

1 *Nature of society and the role of work within it*: every society differs in political, economic and social terms and these forces also change over time. This has an inevitable impact on the approach to managing people across geographic location and time.

2 *Culture*: every society and organisation has a culture that impacts on the way that work is viewed and carried out in that setting. Individual departments and groups within an organisation are also likely to have different cultures which also impacts on work related activity.

3 *Dominant view of people held within the business*: organisations differ in the way that people are viewed and utilised within the business, ranging from a resource to be managed (just like any other), at one extreme, to an equal partner with the owners of the business (if it is a private sector company) at the other. The approach to human resource issues adopted by the management of a particular organisation is determined to a significant extent by their underlying view of people.

4 *Nature of the business*: also impacts on how people management would be practiced within the organisation. For example the provision

of services involving direct interaction between employees and customers require HR practices that attract and retain staff with appropriate capabilities, and also facilitate management's continued encouragement of those behaviours.

5 *Employee reaction to being managed*: employees are human beings and as such are unlike any other resource used within an organisation. They are not totally passive, behaving as expected all of the time. They do not automatically hold the same perceptions and views as managers about the company, what it does and how they are managed.

6 *Impact of legislation on employment relationship*: most countries have legislation which impacts on the rights and responsibilities of managers and employees. This directly shapes many of the human resource management policies and practices adopted.

7 *Individuality*: people differ in their approach to work; in their needs and requirements from the work that they do – and also in what they will tolerate. Some people value high levels of job security over high wages, and some people will articulate problems and others hide their feelings; all of which impact on the ways in which people behave at work.

8 *Group influences*: individuals do not work in isolation, they work in **teams** and groups with other people. They may also be a member of a trade union or professional association. The groups to which people belong can have a significant impact on behaviour at work.

9 *Relative power balance*: there exists a balance of power between the employed and employer which is dependant on many factors in a situation including: skills shortages (or surpluses); economic conditions; level of profitability; changing technology; and government policy. The prevailing power balance between employer and categories of employee can impact on the HR policies and practices adopted.

Useful background reading: material covered in an organisational behaviour or introduction to management course would be relevant support for a fuller understanding of the underlying themes outlined above. One textbook which covers the above themes and a wide range of other topics relevant to the study of human resource management is: Martin (2005) *Organizational Behaviour and Management*.

The curriculum for any course in human resource management will invariably differ between institutions, and in some cases between individual programmes of study at the same institution. You may therefore find that the ordering of topics in the sections below does not exactly match that in your course, but you should be able to find all the topics included here somewhere!

Most human resource lecturers will have preferred topics and academic perspectives that they will emphasise in their courses, and it is also likely that they will have topics and perspectives that they prefer to avoid (or do not have time to cover in detail). You should recognise that and seek to understand the subject matter from the perspective being taught, as that will give you some indication of what to expect in assignments and exams and the key themes that would be expected to be covered in a good answer. More importantly, it will also give you some clues about what NOT to write!

Each section that follows provides a summary of the main issues relevant to that topic, as well as a sample exam question along with an outline of the issues that you should expect to cover in the answer. In using this material you should keep in mind the underlying themes introduced above: referring to appropriate points from these themes in ways relevant to the question asked will usually improve the depth of the discussion in your answer and so almost always gain you marks – provided, of course, that you have not drifted away from the question as set or gone over the required length in an assignment!

2.1	
managing people in a social context	

This section will seek to place the practice of HRM into its broader social, organisational and managerial context. Invariably, just as factors such as society, technology and globalisation have changed over the years, so too has the practice of people management.

Organisations have existed in some form or another since the dawn of collective endeavour in human society. From the earliest days of family and tribal life, the activities of people have had to be directed and channelled in order to increase their chances of survival. Over the centuries human society has changed as knowledge and resources have grown; and human needs, power relationships and culture have evolved. Organisations have also changed over the years as they have adapted to the emerging technologies, relative costs of labour and other resources, markets for products and services, and the prevailing view of work and its role in human life. With even a cursory study of the history of management and organisations, it soon becomes clear that many of the modern management practices have their origins many hundreds – if not thousands – of years ago. For example, it was the Ancient Egyptians who developed centralisation and decentralisation as ways of dealing with organisational complexity around 2000 years BC. The assembly line approach to manufacturing was used for the construction of ships by the Venetians around 1300 AD. For an extended summary of a historical perspective on management and organisations, see Martin (2005: chapter 2).

Over the years the approach to managing people has changed in line with all of the other changes in society and organisations. Personnel management has its direct origins in the nineteenth century as a consequence of recognition by managers and owners of the need to offset the worst aspects of the exploitation of workers that had emerged during the Industrial Revolution. The trade unions were also emerging as a potent force representing workers' rights at about the same time. This could be described as the welfare period in personnel management. Subsequently the emphasis changed and more focus was placed on staffing, training and work organisation – particularly during the First and Second World Wars when, as well as other changes that were taking place, women were first drafted into many jobs traditionally done by men. Since then many other changes such as rising education levels, higher standards of living, attitudes to work, legislation, globalisation and technology have forced organisations to become more sophisticated in the use of people at work; and so personnel management has transformed itself into HRM in order to meet the needs of modern organisations.

Think about it?

To what extent could the emergence of HRM over recent years be described as the latest attempt by managers to find effective ways of controlling workers within the current social environment?

There are four main approaches to explain how the human resource is to be understood in relation to the organisations that employ them.

1 *Resource model*: Developed by Fombrum et al. (1984) this approach holds that human beings are a resource, no different to any other resource within an organisation. Any resource is of value to an organisation providing that it is appropriate, flexible, reliable and cost effective. This approach to HRM begins with the identification of the business strategy which is then converted into HRM strategy, policy and practice in order to deliver the results sought.

2 *Stakeholder model*: Developed by Beer et al. (1984, 1985) this approach takes a stakeholder view of people within organisations. It adopts the same 'top down' business and strategic focus to the role of people as the previous model, but implies that people are more than a static resource to be used as a machine substitute. People represent thinking, dynamic and interactive beings within the organisation. This model stipulates four main areas in which policy is required in order to gain maximum benefit from people: employee influence on management and the business; human resource flow into, out of and within the business; reward systems; and work systems.

3 *Strategy model*: Suggested by Schuler and Jackson (1987, 1996), this model sets out a link between the strategy of the organisation and the employee behaviours necessary to achieve it. They identify two strategy options (representing alternative ways to compete in a particular market) – cost minimisation and innovation – going on to suggest appropriate employee strategies associated with each. For example, cost reduction strategies require: repetitive and predictable behaviours, narrow skill application, and low job involvement. In contrast an innovative strategy requires: a long-term focus, **flexibility** and change, tolerance of ambiguity and uncertainty, and high levels of job involvement among individuals. Relevant HR policies appropriate to the chosen strategy would then be required. What matters is not which approach is used, but that actual HR policy and practices are consistent with the desired strategy.

4 *Interlinked contexts model*: Developed in the UK by Hendry et al. (1989), this model proposes five main interlinked elements that influence how people will be managed in any particular organisational context. They are:

- Outer context: represents the social, economic and cultural forces impacting on the organisation. It also includes organisational issues and influences from the industry and market conditions.
- Inner context: represents the organisational factors that impact on how people are used. For example, its culture, structure, profitability, technology, products or services, management style and politics.

- Business strategy context: represents the effect on people management of the business strategy followed by the organisation.
- Human resource management context: reflects the underlying philosophy of the business about how people should be allowed to contribute to the functioning of the organisation.
- Human resource management content: represents the actual approach to people management in terms of its HRM practices in reward systems, employee relations and work arrangements.

This fourth model demonstrates the complexity of the people management environment for an organisation. The five interacting elements reflect the forces acting upon the situation and which create a dynamic situation which is difficult to manage. One aspect that does not come across strongly in this model is the effect of the individual and groups on the way that HRM is practiced within an organisation. Individuals and groups of employees do not always perceive or understand things in the same way that managers do, and even if they do they may not always wish to comply with management intentions.

This dynamic, personal and complex model supports the view of writers such as Boxall and Purcell (2003) when they suggest that HRM does not 'belong' to specialists because line managers are directly responsible for the management of their subordinates. Consequently everyone within the organisation is actively involved in aspects of people management throughout the working day. In their view the human resource specialist is there to 'sell' their technical expertise to those who have need of support in that area.

Think about it?

What social changes might emerge over the next ten years which might impact on what HRM needs to do? How might work change over the next ten years and what might that mean for the practice of people management?

Possible exam and assignment questions. There are many possible ways in which exam and assignment questions can seek to explore the social context within which HRM is practiced. In general terms there are two main ways in which this topic might be found in a question: first as a support theme for the main discussion purpose of the question and, secondly, as a theme in its own right. An example of the first type of question might be:

"Describe and explain recent trends in the level of trade union membership in Britain."

The answer to this question would be clearly focussed on the general decline in the level of trade union membership in Britain since the early 1980s. However, such a simplistic and bald answer would not address the full meaning of the question (significant reductions in membership levels have occurred before), nor would it tap into the range of possible factors contributing to such a trend. To address such a question fully it would be necessary to include a broader explanation as to why the trend might have arisen. That might include some reference to the historical nature of the employment relationship and changes in legal, political, social and economic factors that have contributed to the current trend. Such a basis would also allow for comparisons with changes in organisational functioning and managerial practice that would be expected to contribute to an explanation of trends in levels of union membership.

An example of the second type of question might be:

"Briefly outline four of the major models of HRM that have been developed and justify which in your view would be more relevant to an explanation of HRM practice in Britain."

The answer to this question would be based strongly on the models outlined above and, in particular, on the Hendry et al. (1989) model because it originated in the UK. To achieve high marks from the answer to such a question it would be necessary to go beyond a description of the four models and to explore the relative contribution of each to an understanding of HR practice in Britain. This implies explaining your reasons for thinking that the Hendry et al. model is a more appropriate reflection of the situation in Britain, not just saying that it is more appropriate because it was developed in that context.

Textbook Guide

ARMSTRONG: *Chapters 1, 3, 11, 14 and 20.*
BEARDWELL, CLAYDON AND BEARDWELL: *Chapters 1 and 3.*
BLOISI: *Chapter 1.*
FOOT AND HOOK: *Chapter 1.*

LEOPOLD, HARRIS AND WATSON: *Chapters 1 and 2.*
MARCHINGTON AND WILKINSON: *Chapter 2.*
PILBEAM AND CORBRIDGE: *Chapter 1.*
REDMAN AND WILKINSON: *Chapters 1 and 9.*
TORRINGTON, HALL AND TAYLOR: *Chapter 1.*

2.2

human resource management and organisations

There are many different types of organisation in terms of size, industry, profitability, purpose, management style and philosophy. In that sense every organisation is different, even by comparison with similar sized organisations within the same industry and based in the same location. The real question is what does 'different' mean in this context? Some writers have explored this issue in terms of culture through the very practical definition of it as 'the ways we do things around here'. However the ways in which organisations differ covers more than the features that would commonly be associated with culture. This section discusses the main features that could be expected to have an impact on how organisations differ and the effect that this might be expected to have on how they manage their human resource.

1 *Industry.* The nature of the product or service from which the organisation derives its income is a primary determinant of the way that an organisation 'organises' itself and consequently how it seeks to manage people in order to achieve its business objectives. For example, a company engaged in manufacturing computers would be expected to differ in many ways from an airline of roughly similar size and age.

2 *Technology.* The type and level of technology used by an organisation both influences and is influenced by the organisation. The use of robots in manufacturing has vastly reduced the need for human involvement in the assembly of products such as motor vehicles. The technology adopted by an organisation is a major influence

on issues such as the number of people employed within an organisation, the types of jobs available and the HR policies necessary to ensure that people contribute effectively to the success of the organisation. Conversely, the type and level of technology used by an organisation is influenced by the people working in it and the business strategies being followed, which also impacts on the approach to people management. For example, the senior management group from a particular department within a company may seek to adopt (or resist the adoption of) a particular technology for political, power or influence reasons rather than business reasons. Equally some organisations trade on the basis of traditional craft manufacturing or the approach to service.

Think about it?

Imagine that you are the senior computer manager of a large insurance company. Further imagine that you know that the introduction of a particular computer based technology could make significant changes to the way the business functions. One side-effect would be to increase the power and significance of the computer department as the business would become even more dependant on it for support and commercial success. However, the new system would result in thousands of job losses in other departments. How might you go about persuading other senior mangers to support your plan?

---

3 *Industry competitive levels.* The degree of competition within an industry significantly influences such factors as product offerings, innovation, prices, customer service and profitability. In essence it reflects the degree of pressure that an organisation is under and so influences senior management decision making. A significant part of the response involves the people aspects of running the business, for example identifying business locations, the number of people employed, and the range of skills required in the future. This might involve a range of HR initiatives including: headcount reductions, **productivity** increases, changing job content, changing skill levels, and maximising the expected levels of **commitment** – all while reducing the cost of labour!

4 *Surrounding political, legislative and cultural context.* Just as each organisation exists within a marketplace for its products and services, each exists within particular political, legal and social context. Each aspect of the environmental context has an impact on how any business can function within that particular setting. For

example, employment legislation has a direct impact on the rights and expectations that each party has in relation to employing people and being employed.

5 *Purpose and philosophy of the organisation.* It is interesting to ask why any particular organisation exists. Some exist to make money for their owners; some to meet defined needs in the market-place; others to meet the employment and career expectations of managers and employees; and others exist to meet identified social, political or cultural needs. Most organisations exist for a mixture of these reasons, whether they are in the public, private or voluntary sectors. Whatever the reason for them being in existence, the purpose and underlying philosophy held by the senior managers and/or owners (politicians in the public sector) will have a significant impact on how the organisation functions and how people are managed within that framework.

6 *Scope of operations.* The scope of activity covered by a specific organisation reflects the breadth of the supply chain embraced. For example, a meat company may incorporate farming, slaughterhouse, meat products factory, transport and distribution, and retail/wholesale food outlets within its operations. Alternatively it may cover only a small part of the entire chain. Whatever the scope of operations embraced by any particular organisation, there would be an impact on a range of HR policies and practices including: recruitment, career development, career opportunities and reward structures.

7 *Patterns of employment.* Attitudes and conventions among managers, employees, politicians and society in general with regard to the length of the working day; number of days worked each week; holidays; shift working; and religious festivals all influence the way in which the workforce and organisations interact. Equally, issues such as equality of employment opportunity and attitudes towards family responsibilities such as caring for the old and young can all influence the patterns of employment undertaken within a particular context.

Think about it?

To what extent is there an inevitable trend over time in developed economies towards people being paid more for working less – leading to high unemployment as jobs inevitably flow to locations with the cheapest labour?

8 *Control processes*. The ways in which the managers of an organisation decide to ensure the objectives they have identified are pursued and achieved also determine, to a significant extent, how employees will be controlled. For example, retail outlets handle a vast array of items that are of value to anyone who can steal them. These include the actual goods being sold, the cash that customers pay, and the credit and debit card details also used by customers. The risk to the business comes not only from external thieves who might attempt to steal in one way or another, but also from employees who may fraudulently divert money or goods. Most retail organisations have very strict rules covering issues such as serving family members and sales to employees, in order to try and minimise employee crime. Control procedures also exist in most organisations covering Internet and email use by staff in an attempt to prevent fraud, access to pornography, and the sending of offensive emails – all such rules being intended to protect the company and its computer systems.

Think about it?

HR practice is about finding the most effective way to control employees in a particular social context. It is about finding the most effective 'iron fist in a velvet glove'. To what extent is this a valid view of HR practice?

---

9 *Employee characteristics*. The people available to be employed within the organisation also bring with them a wide range of characteristics that influence the nature and profile of it. For example, education levels within the general population influences a broad range of issues, including the way that high technology might be used. The general experience of what work means within a particular society will also influence expectations in relation to job design, management style and work ethos.

10 *Organisational structure*. The functional approach to organisational activity in which departments are organised around jobs such as marketing, finance and production requires different HR policies to one which is based upon product groupings with mixed operational teams. For example, in a highly **bureaucratic** organisation HR policies might be targeted at attracting and retaining employees who prefer to follow clear rules and procedures, whereas in an organisation which functions on the basis of **self-managed teams** these policies would not be appropriate.

11 *Management style.* The dominant style of management within the organisation also influences the ways in which people are managed. The use of hierarchical control through layers of supervision and management produces a tall, thin organisational form. This can be contrasted with the approach to management that relies on self-managed work teams and which would provide a 'flatter' organisation as a consequence. With these examples of work organisation, there are clear implications for the approach to management that would offer the highest chance of success and that in turn carries implications for a range of people management practices.

> **Think about it?**
>
> *How might the HR practices differ in a company that adopts an autocratic management style as compared with a company that adopts a democratic management style?*

12 *Work organisation and **job design**.* There are many choices available to management in relation to how the work of an organisation will be structured. For example, the degree of automation adopted, the departmental and work team structures, the level of involvement of employees in decision making and job flexibility all influence the ways in which the various tasks to be completed are combined into the jobs that people actually do. Consequently there are HR issues that arise as a result of these policy decisions, in the areas of recruitment, selection, training, reward and employee relations.

13 *Management preferences and intentions.* Within an organisation the unthinking application of 'standard' HR policies and practices may not produce success because of the differential effects of the factors identified in this discussion list. Managers need to exercise a degree of creativity, preference and choice in designing appropriate HR policies and practices for their organisations and organisational context in ways which enhance commercial success in its broadest sense.

14 *Profitability.* The more profitable an organisation is, the more an elaboration of its structure and functioning becomes possible, creating a direct influence on many aspects of HR policy and practice. For example, highly profitable organisations have an opportunity to increase the number of people employed on a greater range of tasks to the assumed benefit of the organisations. Every manager given an increase in budget could find ways of 'growing their empire' – a training

manager could offer more in-house courses for staff development; a sales manager could achieve higher sales levels by visiting more customers and so on. Equally, the ability to pay million pound bonuses to employees in the financial and legal institutions in the City of London is only possible because of the profitability of those organisations – generated as a result of the number of hours worked by staff, high fee levels and volume of 'billable' hours. So the profitability of an organisation has a direct influence on a range of HR policies and practices.

15 *Organisational culture*. Issues such as the degree of individuality expected from employees and the formality of interpersonal interaction at work are just some of the cultural influences on the way that work is undertaken within an organisation. In addition there is an inevitable tension within large international organisations between the need for a global corporate identity and the dominant culture within local operating environments. There is considerable effort within HR functions these days to engender appropriate cultures – appropriate, that is, to management determined objectives – usually based around the notion of high performance working. HR policies and practices aimed at increasing the commitment (often described as 'buy-in') of employees to management objectives seek to make clear the benefits to employees arising from delivering the expected behaviours.

Think about it?

High performance working is nothing more than a management attempt to get more work from employees without having to pay for it. Do you agree with this view? Why or why not?

---

16 *Location*. There are cultural, legislative and dominant business practice issues that vary across the world and which shape organisations within their national borders. Aspects such as communications and transportation also influence activities significantly. For example, mining operations are frequently carried out far from the location of the users of the extracted minerals and the company head office. The impact of these issues on HR policy and practice arises from the variety in operational activity and locational difference. For example, the HR practices appropriate for a company HQ based in Paris might be totally, different to those required in a manufacturing facility based in Shanghai, and different again for a sales office based in London.

17 *Size*. The physical size of an organisation is a major determinant of how it functions. The small corner shop selling a range of grocery items and sweets, employing two people, would be vastly different in terms of its HR requirements when compared to a large national supermarket chain with many thousands of employees. The size of an organisation could also influence many of the other variables, such as the level of technology that it is able to support, profitability and control processes – all of which impact on HR policy and practice.

18 *Age and history*. There is an apparent stability and security that comes from the appearance of age – financial institutions deliberately create this image for commercial purposes. The age of an organisation could also be expected to impact on many structural and functional issues that might impact on HR policy and practice. For example, many employees with long service may remember aspects of company tradition and resist attempts to 'modernise' methods of working unless innovation and change is already the norm.

Think about it?

Talk to parents, friends or anyone you know who has worked in the same organisation for more than five years and discuss any changes that have taken place in relation to HR policy and practice. See if you can identify any of the factors discussed above as influences in those changes.

Possible exam and assignment questions: There are many possible ways in which exam and assignment questions can seek to explore the organisational context within which HRM is practiced. In general terms there are two main ways in which this topic might be found in a question: first as a support theme for the main discussion purpose of the question and, secondly, as a theme in its own right. An example of the first type of question might be:

❝Describe and explain how HR policy might be determined within an organisation.❞

The answer to this question would be seeking to explore issues around how organisations develop their HR policies – a topic appropriate to Section 2.12 later. Also relevant to this type of answer would be material from Section 2.1 – on models of HR in relation to organisations and the surrounding context. Equally, material from this section has relevance to the question as set and any of the factors mentioned in this section could be introduced and briefly discussed as support for the way that policy is determined and some of the influences on that process.

An example of the second type of question might be:

"Briefly outline and justify four of the factors that might be expected to influence HR policy and practice within a multi-site geographically dispersed financial services organisation."

The answer to this question would be based on any of the factors discussed above. The key points in answering the question are to outline what each factor means and how it might influence HR policy (shows basic understanding of the topics) and then to justify how each factor would be relevant to the type of organisation indicated. For example, in such international financial services organisations the surrounding political, legislative and cultural context impacting on each location might be expected to have an impact on HR policy; similarly, the political and cultural based expectations with regard to 'localisation' or the employment of local (as opposed to expatriate) labour at every location have to be managed – all within the need to maintain cohesive and consistent corporate level policy and practice.

Textbook Guide

ARMSTRONG: *Chapters 3, 10 and 20.*
BEARDWELL, CLAYDON AND BEARDWELL: *Chapters 2 and 3.*
BLOISI: *Chapter 1.*
FOOT AND HOOK: *Chapter 1.*
LEOPOLD, HARRIS AND WATSON: *Chapters 1, 2 and 11.*
MARCHINGTON AND WILKINSON: *Chapters 2 and 4.*
PILBEAM AND CORBRIDGE: *Chapter 1.*
REDMAN AND WILKINSON: *Chapter 1.*
TORRINGTON, HALL AND TAYLOR: *Chapter 1.*

2.3

the legal context, including contracts of employment

There exists a legal basis to the employment of people by an organ-isation and this section will seek to introduce the major themes of this aspect of HRM policy and practice. Specific statutes relating to **employment legislation** are enacted by Parliament in the UK (including the devolved Parliament in Scotland and the Welsh Assembly) and through provisions originating from European Union Law. The common law also has a significant impact on HR policy and practice, and establishes the basic duties and responsi-bilities of both employer and employee. Case law continually adapts and clarifies statutory provision in the light of particular circumstances presented to superior courts, which then become binding on the judgments of the lower courts (**Employment Tribunals**). Inevitably, therefore, the discussion of any aspect of employment legislation will be out of date to some degree as soon as it is written.

Is someone an employee or not seems to be a simple question. Yet it is both complex to answer and important to do so as employees have more rights in law than non-employees. Some employers have deliberately sought to minimise their responsibilities to employees by seeking to classify workers as self-employed. Ultimately only the courts can provide a definitive answer to the question but at a commonsense level it comes down to employees having a '**contract of service**', whereas non-employees work under a '**contract for services**'.

Think about it?

What are the differences between the terms 'contract of service' and 'contract for services'?

Employee and worker rights include:

Table 3.1

Some of the rights that apply only to employees	Some of the rights that apply to all workers
• Right to a statement of terms and conditions of employment • Right to an itemised pay statement • Statutory sick pay • Time off for public duties • Trade union rights • Minimum notice periods • Maternity/paternity leave and pay rights • Unfair dismissal rights	• Equal pay for equal work • Non-discrimination on the grounds of sex, race, religious belief, sexual orientation and disability • Health and safety rights • Minimum wage and working time rights • Data protection rights • Carer's responsibility rights

The main obligations of employers and employees under the common law are listed in Table 3.2

Table 3.2   Comman law obligations butween employer and employee

Owed by employer to the employees	Owed by employees to the employer
• Duty of care • Duty to pay agreed wages • Duty to provide work • Duty not to treat employees in an arbitrary or vindictive way • Duty to provide support to employees • Duty to provide safe systems of work • Duty to maintain relationship of mutual trust and confidence	• Duty to cooperate with employer • Duty to obey reasonable/lawful instructions • Duty to exercise reasonable care and skill in duties performed • Duty to act in good faith • Duty of fidelity (also applies to ex-employees) • Duty to maintain relationship of mutual trust and confidence

A contract of employment does not have to be written to exist, although it is preferable if it does; this is why legislation provides that employees must be provided with a statement of the main terms and conditions of employment. The document is not a contract as such, just a statement of the main terms. The totality of the contract will include things that are usual 'custom and practice' within the organisation, elements from both the common and statute law, and also (if it is applicable) agreements with trade unions, staff associations, trade associations and so on which might determine such things as pay review practices and their timings. A contract comes into existence when an offer is made by one party and is accepted by the other. Once formed, the contract cannot be unilaterally changed by either party without the agreement of the other. However, as with many such matters, it is not quite as simple as this explanation might imply. For example, an employer might argue that it is essential for the survival of the organisation to cut wages and so seek to impose a wage cut on employees. Employees are then faced with the options of seeking legal redress for breach of contract; taking some form of industrial action; or accepting the change. In seeking to change contract terms, an employer may give notice to terminate the existing employee contract and offer continued employment based on changed terms and conditions of employment. If not accepted then employment would be terminated and the employee would be forced to seek legal redress if they felt aggrieved by the decision.

In addition to the contract of employment there is much emphasis these days on the **psychological contract**. The psychological contract refers to the unspoken and unwritten expectations that both parties have in relation to the role and responsibilities of the other party in the employment relationship. It is argued that the traditional psychological contract is changing although the evidence is far from clear. The differences between the old and new psychological contracts are highlighted in Table 3.3.

Table 3.3

Traditional psychological contract	Evolving psychological contract
• Work hard on behalf of employer	• I will contribute creatively and with appropriate effort
• Act loyally towards employer	• I don't expect/want long term employment
• Work in best interests of the employer	• I expect development to be provided to maintain and enhance my market worth
• Expect long-term employment in return	• I will take personal responsibility for my career
• Expect development and career advancement should the opportunity arise	• I expect a salary commensurate with my contribution and market worth

Think\ about it?

It has been suggested that the psychological contract is much more important to the employment relationship than the formal contract of employment. Why might this be so and to what extent do you agree with that opinion?

The major areas of legislation (in addition to contracts of employment) which have a direct influence on HR practice are discussed below.

Wages and working hours

The Equal Pay Act (1970), as subsequently amended, seeks to ensure that men and women are paid on the basis of the requirements of the work that they do rather than on the basis of their gender. It seeks to eliminate unjustified wage differences and provides for independent experts to guide the courts in reaching conclusions on such matters. There is also provision in legislation to prevent employees having unauthorised deductions taken from their pay, with special provision being made for workers in retail employment who may be subject to deductions to cover stock or cash shortages. Employers are allowed to make some deductions from pay automatically, including income tax and National Insurance (NI) and where the employee has given prior consent, or if it is to recover previous overpayment. There is also the existence of **minimum wage** legislation which sets the lowest level permissible for both young employees and adults. The **Working Time Directive** was introduced across Europe as a health and safety measure, in an attempt to ensure that no employee was forced against their will to work more than 48 hours in any week. The UK currently allows an opt out of that requirement if employees agree to work more than the maximum 48 hours per week allowed under the regulations. The European Commission is currently seeking to make changes to the opt out rules.

Recognition of trade unions and consultation

Although trade union membership has declined significantly over recent years they are far from being an insignificant force. Although unions have some legal rights to require employers to recognise them for the purposes of representing employees and collective bargaining, these are seldom used. Faced with a claim from a trade union for **recognition** a management has several options open to it. It can refuse, or seek to negotiate an agreement that would provide an acceptable form of recognition. Even if no formal recognition agreement exists it might still be possible for a union to argue that it is entitled to the statutory rights under law as a result of 'custom and practice' within the company, for example, if talks over proposed **redundancy** had taken place with a union official in the past. With recognition comes the right of trade union members and officers to not be discriminated against and for certain time off rights for appropriate union duties. In relation to consultation there are many situations that confer the right for trade unions to be consulted including issues relating to:

- Redundancy.
- Health and safety.
- Transfer of undertakings.
- Pensions.
- European Works Councils (in relevant 'community scale' operations).
- Workplace agreements.
- Information and Consultation Directive.

Data protection rights

The Information Commissioner oversees legislative provision for the personal data collected by any organisation and its use – known as **data protection**. There are a number of principles governing the processing of personal data including:

- Personal data shall be processed fairly and lawfully.
- Personal data shall be obtained only for specified and lawful purposes, and shall not be processed in any manner incompatible with those purposes.
- Personal data shall be adequate, relevant and not excessive in relation to the purposes for which it is processed.
- Personal data shall be accurate and, where necessary, kept up to date.
- Personal data shall be kept for no longer than is necessary for the purposes for which it is processed.
- Personal data shall be processed in accordance with the rights of data subjects under the Data Protection Act.

- Personal data shall be subject to appropriate technical and organisational measures to protect against unauthorised or unlawful processing and accidental loss, destruction or damage.
- Personal data shall not be transferred to a country or territory outside the European Economic Area unless that country or territory ensures an adequate level of data protection.

Employees have the right to access data held on them and to make corrections if they feel it to be incorrect. They also have the right to seek redress through the courts if they feel that their rights have been abused.

Health, safety and welfare

The basic statutory protection in place is the Health and Safety at Work Act (1974) which is supplemented by more recent legislation covering such issues as the Control of Substances Hazardous to Health Regulations (COSHH) of 1988. There is also legislation covering issues such as violence at work; and requirements for fire prevention, ventilation, sanitary facilities, safety signs and the setting up of safety committees. In addition there are various requirements originating from Europe covering issues such as noise control, manual handling of heavy loads, use of visual display units, and also the control of carcinogenic and biological agents. The Health and Safety Commission is responsible for the oversight and enforcement of health and safety within organisations and it also issues Codes of Practice which, although not legally enforceable, set the standards against which actions and behaviour are judged. Employees as well as employers have responsibilities under health and safety legislation and are equally liable to be prosecuted for a failure to comply with appropriate requirements.

Disability and sick pay rights

The Equality and Human Rights Commission that holds the remit to act on issues relating to **discrimination** against disabled people. The legislation seeks to prevent an employer directly discriminating against (or victimising) a disabled person. The term 'disabled' in the Disability Discrimination Act (DDA) has been given a very broad meaning in relation to 'physical or mental impairment' and also employers are required to make 'reasonable adjustment' in accommodating the needs of the employee.

Statutory sick pay is a benefit paid by the state to employees who are unable to go to work because of illness. The levels of payment and the conditions under which it is paid are covered by regulation, and it is administered by employers through the normal payroll system. The statutory system has no direct bearing on any occupational scheme that an employer may decide to operate; it simply provides a minimum standard which employers must follow.

Maternity, paternity and carer's rights

In relation to maternity and paternity there are statutory rights both to leave and to pay covering the period before the birth (mothers) and subsequent to it (mothers and fathers). There is also a statutory right for expectant mothers to attend ante-natal care provision. Similar rights extend to adoption leave.

Employees also have a right to request flexible working hours to care for young children and certain advits in need of care. Employers can refuse the request under certain prescribed conditions. There is also the right to take reasonable time off work because of urgent family reasons. For example, because of the break down of the usual arrangements to care for a dependent relative.

Equality

There are a wide range of areas in which legislation has sought to provide fairness – **equality** – in the work relationship, including seeking to prevent employers from taking decisions about people on grounds that are irrelevant to the purpose of the decision. For example, in recruitment and selection it should be in the employer's interests to hire the best person for the job; it should not make any difference (in terms of job requirements) whether the applicant is black or white, male or female, and so on.

Think about it?

To what extent can legislation change attitudes and behaviour in relation to equality?

The range of issues covered under anti-discrimination legislation includes:

- Sex.
- Race.
- Marital status.
- Ethnic or national origin.
- Disability.
- Sexual orientation.
- Age.
- Religious beliefs.
- Union membership (or non-membership).
- Part-time or fixed-term contract workers.
- Ex-offenders with spent convictions.

Grievance and discipline

There exists a requirement for organisations to have appropriate **grievance** and disciplinary policies and procedures in place; if they do not, then the courts will expect the statutory procedures to be followed. **Disciplinary procedures** cover situations in which the employer has the need to take an employee to task for failing to work or behave in an appropriate manner. Grievance procedures exist so that if the employee feels that they have been unfairly treated by the employer (or another employee) they have a means of seeking redress or of having the 'problem' dealt with.

Termination of employment

All employment comes to an end at some point in time. That can be as a result of either party giving notice to the other within the terms of the contract of employment, or as a result of redundancy, the death or retirement of the employee, the collapse of the company, or the unilateral termination of the contract (without notice) by either party. Existing legislation provides for the employee who feels that their employment has been terminated for an unfair reason or in an unfair manner to have the right to make application to an Employment Tribunal for their case to be heard and if upheld to receive redress from the employer.

Enforcement

Many of the legislative rights outlined above carry the right for an employee to go to an Employment Tribunal to seek redress for the breach of their rights. In doing so there is the opportunity for either party to take advantage of the services offered by ACAS (Advisory, Conciliation and Arbitration Service) who will seek to conciliate a settlement between the parties before a full Tribunal case is heard.

Think about it?

To what extent could it be argued that HRM has emerged as a response to the changing labour market, including the role of employment legislation, and the resulting need to have a management discipline with specialist skills in managing people within that complex framework?

Possible exam and assignment questions. There are many possible ways in which exam and assignment questions can seek to explore the legal context surrounding HRM. The two main ways in which this topic might be found in a question are introduced here: first as a support theme for the main discussion purpose of the question and, secondly, as a theme in its own right. An example of the first type of question might be:

"What is a psychological contract and how might it differ from the written contract of employment?"

The answer to this question would require a description of both the psychological contract and the written contract of employment. In doing so it would be important to draw a distinction between the contract of employment as a legal entity and the 'written statement of main terms and conditions of employment' that most people would receive when they start a new job. The idea that a contract of employment is based on a range of rights and obligations for both parties should form the basis of the discussion, with the psychological contract being that part of the overall employment relationship which is based on the unspoken and unwritten expectations that both parties have in relation to the role and responsibilities of the other party. The discussion about the degree to which research suggests that the psychological contract is changing would also form a useful element in the answer.

An example of the second type of question might be:

"Outline the legislative provision in relation to equality of opportunity and briefly justify one new piece of legislation that you would wish to see introduced to strengthen equality of opportunity in a specific area of your choice."

The answer to this question would be based on a brief review of the current legislative provision covering areas including sex, equal pay, race, ethnicity, religious belief, sexual orientation, age, disability and marital status. Based on your understanding of the current social situation and the relative effectiveness of the legislation, you should select an area on which to propose (with justification) new legislation. For example, equal pay for work of equal value could be argued to have been largely ineffective in eliminating the gender pay difference so there may be scope for revised legislative provision. Of course you could argue that it is not possible to eliminate discrimination through legislation, so that no new legislation should be introduced. However, although this might be justified it is not directly in alignment with the question and so might be penalised by the marker – it is a risk strategy to approach the question in this way without more specific guidance from your lecturer!

Textbook Guide

ARMSTRONG: *Chapters 31 and 57.*
BEARDWELL, CLAYDON AND BEARDWELL: *Chapter 12.*
BLOISI: *Various chapters make some reference to this topic.*
FOOT AND HOOK: *Chapter 5.*
LEOPOLD, HARRIS AND WATSON: *Chapters 3 and 14.*
MARCHINGTON AND WILKINSON: *Various chapters make some reference to this topic.*
REDMAN AND WILKINSON: *Various chapters make some reference to this topic.*
TORRINGTON, HALL AND TAYLOR: *Chapters 5, 9, 22, 23, 24 and 25.*

2.4

HR planning, resourcing and retention

Important questions for any organisation are:

- How many people do we require?
- When do we need them?
- What range of competencies do we require now and in the future?
- How do we keep the people that we need?
- What do we do when we have more people than we need?

Once an organisation knows what it wants to do in terms of its business activities it is then in a position to convert this information into its requirements for people. **Resourcing** represents an expensive and time-consuming activity so it makes sense to hang on to people for as long as possible. But inevitably at some point people will leave – for a range of reasons. This section of your Companion will discuss these important HR processes.

HR Planning

It is important to recognise that **HR planning** represents an ongoing, dynamic process involving an organisation that is already in existence with a defined business activity and an established level of staffing. Business strategy and planning therefore represent continuous processes intended to provide direction and certainty in an uncertain environmental context. Only on the creation of a new business of some size would the processes discussed here be used for the first time.

The traditional approach to HR planning sought to identify the gap between labour requirements and availability, and then to develop strategies to deal with the discrepancy. It achieved this in a semi-mechanical way by the following measures:

- Converting future business plans into projected labour requirements. This involved the breakdown of projected labour by such variables as location, grade and **skill**.

- The creation of a profile of the existing workforce was also required using variables such as the number of people employed by grade, working hours, age, skill and location.
- It was also necessary to understand what labour was available from external labour markets.
- HR planning involved the reconciliation of the first two items above (requirement and existing availability). The labour plans that emerged might suggest the need for additional (or fewer) people.

At that time there was little by way of retraining or flexibility envisaged because the comparative cost would be excessive (compared to labour replacement); there were job demarcation issues (tight restrictions on who could undertake what tasks); and restricted entry to many jobs limited the possibilities.

HR planning is now more sophisticated and complex, and would envisage more of a cyclical and interactive process involving the answers to questions such as:

- What business are we currently in?
- Where are we now in relation to that business strategy?
- Where do we, as a business, want to be in the future?
- How do we get there?
- How do we reshape what we have now into what we want in the future?
- How do we handle the transition?

These are very general and open-ended questions, with the answers liable to change frequently as the numerous variables acting on the organisation change. For example, the sudden and unanticipated entry of a competitor product or service into the marketplace might be expected to have a major impact on business strategy in both the short and the long term. The answers to these open-ended questions about the business and how it positions itself relative to the world in which it operates are essential to an understanding of the current and future need for people. It is not just an understanding of how many people are needed, or when, or of the skills that they will need that results from such an approach to HR planning. The approach encourages a more creative and holistic approach to the determination of how people can contribute to the long-term success of the organisation. The earlier approach encouraged a mechanistic matching of numbers required and numbers available across time. The HRM approach seeks to encourage the adoption of a dynamic interaction between people and organisational objectives in the light of the ever-changing reality of operational activity. Of course, the same basic data and understanding of labour markets and demographics is required in both approaches; the difference is in how that information is used and integrated into the management of people.

The outcomes from the HR planning process include a range of more specific HR plans or intentions covering such areas as:

- Resourcing plans.
- Organisation design plans.
- People utilisation plans.
- Training and development plans.
- Performance management and motivation plans.
- Reward plans.
- Employee relations plans.

Think about it?

To what extent is the above approach to HR planning a response to the changing social, political and economic environments within which business must operate?

Resourcing

Resourcing covers three main areas of HR activity: recruitment, **selection** and appointment.

Recruitment

This part of the resourcing process is about bringing forward an appropriate pool of potentially appropriate candidates from which a specific selection of individual(s) will be interviewed. As such it consists of a number of steps:

1 *Identification of a vacancy.* People leave and new posts are created all the time in organisations, but that does not automatically mean that recruitment needs to be undertaken. Posts can be eliminated, filled by redesigning the jobs, or by sub-contracting, for example. For each vacancy it is necessary to create a **job description** and a **person specification** identifying the key attributes of the job and someone undertaking it.

2 *Labour markets*. Having identified the need to fill a vacancy it is necessary to identify where likely candidates might be found. That involves understanding the labour markets appropriate to the position(s). In some cases that may be internal to the company, or they can be external. There are many possible external labour markets; for example, some jobs will attract people living locally whereas others may involve specialised skills and experience and candidates may be based across the world.

3 *Advertising*. This is about accessing appropriate labour markets in order to bring the job opportunity to the attention of as many potential applicants as possible. The aim is to attract enough high calibre applicants but not so many average or inferior candidates that it 'swamps' the selection process. It represents a creative process involving many decisions about where to place the advert, the style of the advert, and the information contained in it.

Think about it?

Produce an advert for the job of a university lecturer in HRM. Compare your advert with some actual adverts for jobs of that type. If they differ, why might that be and how would you seek to justify that yours is superior to the real adverts?

4 *Documentation*. A range of documents is necessary for any resourcing process including: job and person specification; advert; vacancy/advert authorisation and sign-off approvals; decide on use of **curriculum vitae (CV)** or standard application forms; staff handbooks and any relevant contracts/agreements; application tracking log; standard letters covering the stages of the process; and shortlisting criteria.

5 *Initial sifting*. Once the applications are available to the company it will be necessary to systematically grade the applications so that eventually three 'piles' emerge. The three piles are: definitely interview, possibly interview, and reject. Sifting is a critical stage in the process and can be difficult if there are a large number of applications or, alternatively, very few applications. There are no rules about how many people should progress to the next round – selection – but it is a dynamic process that takes time. It is also likely that applicants will have applied for jobs with other organisations and will be at different stages of the process with each. Consequently, a degree of drop-out in the process can be expected. The people involved in the sifting process should be line managers and HR specialists, and

their aim should be to identify an objective method of differentiating between candidates in relation to the requirements of the vacancy. The goal is to select the best candidates while avoiding discrimination or bias creeping into the process – deliberately or accidentally.

Selection

This represents a two-way process and is as much about the applicant selecting the organisation as it is about the organisation selecting the applicant. If the process; people; organisation; **job**; terms and conditions of work; job/career prospects for the individual do not all come across as positive during the process the individual is likely to reject the job, even if it is offered to them. It has been argued that from the organisation's perspective there are three levels of 'fit' that are being evaluated during the selection process:

- Fit with the organisation.
- Fit with the department and team.
- Fit with the job itself.

There are many selection methods that can be used as part of the selection process. The choice of methods will depend on many factors including, appropriateness, numbers involved, time and cost. They include:

- Application form or CV.
- Interviews.
- Self and peer assessment.
- Telephone interviews.
- **Psychometric testing.**
- Group methods and **assessment centres.**
- Work tests and portfolios.
- References.
- Other methods such as handwriting analysis.

Appointment

The final stage of the selection process should be the identification of the chosen applicant(s) for the job(s) being filled. In an ideal world the chosen individual would be contacted with a formal offer of employment, they would accept it and a starting date would be determined. However, it is never that simple as an individual may reject an offer immediately or at any time before starting work – or even shortly after starting work (the induction crisis). Equally things can change for the company and it may find itself in a position of having to withdraw the offer of a job. It represents a 'dangerous' time for both parties and as a consequence it is likely that both will have some contingency plans. For example, some organisations delay notifying rejected applicants so that they have the possibility of making one of them an offer if necessary. However this can only last for a few days as applicants will be sensitive to any delay in notification and so become aware that they were 'second best', with all that is implied by such a perception! On the other hand applicants may continue with any outstanding applications and only make a decision when they feel it necessary to make a binding commitment.

Think about it?

What is the 'induction crisis' and how can it be avoided?

Other resourcing options

Another area of decision making is in relation to the role of a **recruitment agency** or employment consultant. Such providers claim to offer a professional, cost-effective and efficient service. They can advertise either using the company details or anonymously if it is a sensitive recruitment situation. The range of services includes:

- Assistance with the creation, layout and placing of adverts.
- Assistance with the creation of job and personnel specifications.
- Developing a role brief; developing person specification; advertising; and drawing up a shortlist for selection.
- Additional services could include psychometric testing and initial interviews.

Think about it?

Why might an organisation wish to advertise vacancies without revealing who they are?

Retention

Having appointed an individual to a position it would be hoped that they will wish to remain with it. However, sometimes situations arise where either party realises that they have made a mistake and would seek to end the employment relationship as quickly and painlessly as possible.

People leave organisations for many reasons and, equally, organisations release people for a variety of reasons too. These include:

- Increased income.
- Better job/career prospects or promotion.
- Change type of work.
- To gain experience.
- Change industry.
- Family/career responsibilities.
- To work fewer hours or change work pattern.
- Dissatisfaction with current job/company/working conditions.
- To escape poor working relationships with boss and/or colleagues.
- Retirement.
- Death or serious illness.
- Family or company moving location.
- Company closure or redundancy.
- Change in company fortunes.

Some of the common staff **retention** strategies include:

- *Managing expectation* about the job, company and career development prior to appointment. If the reality of the work experience does not match the employee expectation then it is likely that they will become dissatisfied and leave.
- *Reward.* Most individuals would say that they are worth more money and would take it if offered. In practical terms the feeling of being paid fairly and equitably can go a long way to helping employees feel valued.
- ***Induction***. Induction is about 'converting' a new recruit into an effective member of the organisation as quickly and effectively as possible. If the induction process is missing or not effective then the new person will feel lost, unsure of their role and an outsider. They will inevitably question their decision to join the company and may have outstanding applications that could lead to alternative offers of employment.
- *Work-life balance and family-friendly HR practices.* People have many responsibilities including childcare, elder care, or other family commitments. It can also include voluntary and other commitments that people acquire over the course of their lives and which mean that work is not the only important commitment they have. Consequently the greater flexibility and creativity that a company applies to meeting the needs of people across all aspects of their lives, then the more likely they are to retain them and to achieve an effective contribution and performance.
- ***Training and development***. Not everyone seeks **promotion** to more senior jobs, but there are always ways in which people can grow and develop. Meeting those desires helps to 'bind' employees to the organisation.

- *Good management*. The higher the quality of line management, the more effective will be many aspects of operational activity. This encourages employees to feel 'connected' to the organisation and valued by it, so aiding retention.

Think about it?

What might good managers do that poor managers do not that would positively impact on retention of employees?

- *Job and organisational design*. Boring, monotonous, meaningless work is less likely to hold the interest of employees beyond the need for an income. Interesting work with well-designed jobs within an effective organisation structure is likely to retain employees for longer.
- *Employee relations policies*. Employee involvement and participation in decision making represent ways in which individuals can contribute and gain an understanding of issues that they would not normally encounter. Such policies seek to ensure that employee contribution is valued and captured to the benefit of both parties, and in so doing can enhance the value gained by employees so aiding retention.

Dealing with a surplus of people

So far resourcing has been about acquiring and holding on to people once the 'need' has been identified. However, there are circumstances when a surplus of people will be identified. It would be hoped that this problem could be identified far enough ahead to enable appropriate resourcing strategies to be developed in order to avoid the need to reduce the number of people employed. But this may not always be the case. The need to deal with a surplus of people could be minimised or avoided by the adoption of a number of strategies including:

- Retraining.
- Slowing recruitment.
- Seeking/adopting new business opportunities.
- Marketing strategies.
- Encouragement of **secondments**; **sabbaticals**; family-friendly working; flexible working; flexible reward strategies; use of sub-contractors and other forms of **peripheral working**.
- Phased retirement.

Once it becomes a necessity, there are a number of ways in which a surplus can be dealt with. However it is achieved it must be remembered that it will have an impact on the company reputation and possibly its customers/sales levels. The reputation (employer brand) gained by a company during such reduction processes can significantly impact on its future ability to attract good quality applicants. The ways to reduce the numbers employed (after appropriate consultation with relevant trade unions) include any one or combination of the following:

- *Voluntary redundancy*. Seeking people who wish to leave the organisation under a **voluntary redundancy** scheme, probably on enhanced terms, can be one way of reducing the number employed. The problem with it is that it invites individuals to self select and consequently those with long service and/or transferable skills may see it as a way of gaining a significant sum of money with the opportunity to move easily into another job. It is most attractive to the people that the organisation may want and/or need to retain. The option of management retaining the right to reject an applicant may seem attractive but such a rejection may seriously demotivate individuals.
- *Enforced redundancy*. This may seem attractive as it involves the selection of those least valuable to the future success of the business using appropriate criteria. There are many selection criteria that could be used, but it is not easy to identify the 'best' criteria for all circumstances. Last-in, first-out (**LIFO**) can be the cheapest but may identify some individual that the employer may wish to retain, and miss employees of long service who may not be effective performers. Performance is notoriously difficult to define and measure in a way that would not fall foul of legislation or of employee opinion.
- *Short-time working*. There are many variations on **short-time working**, from people working (and being paid) for working fewer days each month, to the introduction of part-time working and job share as a way of keeping people employed but with them doing less work overall.
- *Early retirement*. This option can be very expensive but can have similar benefits – and difficulties – to voluntary redundancy.
- *Sabbaticals*. This option would allow individuals to take a break from the company and their career for a specified period of time. Individuals might want to study, go travelling, work for a charity or any number of things given the time to do so and the opportunity to return to their job. It would be useful in situations where a surplus had been identified as being an event lasting for a relatively short period.
- *Secondments/transfers*. This would be similar to the sabbatical but might involve a planned programme of seconding individuals to other parts of the group, or to charities or to other organisations facing a shortage of particular skills or in need of an injection of broader skills.
- ***Delayed appointment***. Having gone through an extensive resourcing process and made appointments, organisations have occasionally been faced with a crisis and the need to cut staff. For example, graduates waiting to begin their first jobs have been offered money to wait a year to start work.

However a surplus of people is dealt with it is necessary to try to retain a positive climate of employee relations. It is not just the employees leaving who must be handled fairly but those remaining must also be considered; after all, it is they who will have to keep the organisation functioning afterwards. It is necessary to ensure that legislation is complied with throughout the process of reducing the numbers employed as litigation is an expensive process and can also significantly impact on the employer brand.

Possible exam and assignment questions. There are many possible ways in which exam and assignment questions can seek to explore resourcing issues within HRM. The two main ways in which this topic might be found in a question are introduced here: first as a support theme for the main discussion purpose of the question and, secondly, as a theme in its own right. An example of the first type of question might be:

"Discuss the extent to which HR strategy and corporate strategy are linked."

The answer to this question would require a discussion of both HR and corporate strategy and how they are linked. Relevant to that discussion would be the approach identified at the start of this section in relation to HR planning. It would also be useful to introduce aspects of recruitment, selection, retention and reduction into the discussion as this might support the points being made about the importance to the organisation of linking its approach to, and actual management of, people to what it seeks to achieve in business terms. The material in Section 12 would also be relevant.

An example of the second type of question might be:

"Outline the main features of an organisation's resourcing practice."

The answer to this question would be based on the major elements included in this section. It would include a brief discussion of HR planning which would lead to the specific practices of:

- Recruitment.
- Selection.
- Appointment.

In addition it could be useful to introduce aspects of retention and dealing with surplus employees, as appropriate to the flow of the discussion.

Textbook Guide

ARMSTRONG: *Chapters 13, 15, 16, 25, 26, 27, 28, 29 and 30.*
BEARDWELL, CLAYDON AND BEARDWELL: *Chapters 4 and 5.*
BLOISI: *Chapters 2, 4 and 5.*
FOOT AND HOOK: *Chapters 2, 3, 4 and 5.*
LEOPOLD, HARRIS AND WATSON: *Chapter 6.*
MARCHINGTON AND WILKINSON: *Chapter 6.*
PILBEAM AND CORBRIDGE: *Chapters 3, 4, 6 and 7.*
REDMAN AND WILKINSON: *Chapter 3.*
TORRINGTON, HALL AND TAYLOR: *Chapters 3, 6, 7 and 8.*

2.5	
training and development	

Organisations need to adapt to changing circumstances; consequently there exists a requirement to constantly train and develop employees and managers to be able to continue to perform effectively. The approach to training and development activity also indicates what management believe to be important, including their attitude towards customers and employees.

Learning

Learning represents the underlying process that an individual goes through when they acquire a new way of doing (or understanding) something. It is therefore fundamental to any training or development activity within an organisation.

How people learn has long been an area of interest in psychology and a number of models have developed which seek to explain it. They include:

1 *Behaviourist models.* These represent the earliest models (developed by researchers including Pavlov and Skinner) and are based on the reinforcement of desired behaviours through the application of rewards to the individual who displays them. In this approach to learning, the individual 'acquires' the behaviour patterns that the 'trainer' seeks to instil in them – assuming that they want the reward associated with performing as required! They are widely used in organisations through the use of productivity (or performance) based bonus schemes. Meeting targets set by a superior is used as the basis of deciding bonus payments, promotion and even salary levels for many employees, including senior managers and directors.

2 *Cognitive models.* This approach is based on providing the individual with the cognitive frameworks to enable them to interact more effectively with the environment around them. The early insights into this approach were based on trial and error learning in which a chimpanzee was placed in a box with a short stick in reach, with a banana and long stick out of reach. After a while studying the 'problem' (including a number of attempts that failed to reach the food) the chimpanzee suddenly used the short stick to pull the long stick into reach and then used that to pull the banana into reach. The animal had used cognitive problem-solving processes to 'learn' how to obtain the food. Information processing approaches are a development of this basic model. They suggest that the problem-solving process contains the following elements and stages:

- Previous experience and learning.
- Present situation analysis.
- Identification of behaviour options (how the individual might respond to the current problem).
- Behaviour choice (the actual response to the identified problem).
- Perceived outcome (what happens to the problem and surrounding issues as a result of the actual behaviour).
- Result and consequences added to the individual's learning, knowledge and experience (to enable future problems to be solved more easily).

This process uses feedback as a significant part of the learning process.

3 *Social learning models.* This approach is based on the observation that people are socialised into various groups throughout their lives. For example, children are brought up within family units, and new employees are inducted into departments and the jobs that they will be performing. Consequently individuals need to 'learn' what is expected of them in order to achieve integration within each of these groups. This approach to learning reflects the ways in which

that need is met through the 'programmed experience' provided by the various parents, peers, guides and mentors involved.

4 *Experiential learning models.* The Kolb learning cycle is the best known of these and consists of a four-stage process for learning to be effective. These stages are:

- Experience. This can either be a planned or unplanned event that the individual becomes involved with.
- Reflection. As the result of the experience the individual is able to consider such issues as what has happened, why and how they responded to it.
- Generalisation. The result of thinking about the experience is an ability to envisage the results being applicable to other situations.
- Experimentation. This represents the opportunity to apply the result of generalisation to actual situations; the consequence of which is to begin another cycle of the model through another experience to reflect upon.

Among the implications of this model is that learning represents an ongoing process that will happen in the course of everyday experience of each individual.

Think about it?

One consequence of the Kolb model is an understanding that if managers do not undertake the training of employees, then it takes place anyway – and in ways that management cannot control! What might that imply?

Each of the four stages in the Kolb model has become linked to a particular learning style preference identified by writers such as Honey and Mumford (1989). They are:

- Activist. Such individuals prefer action and learn best from doing something.
- Reflector. Such individuals prefer to understand what they are trying to achieve based on observation, their experience and that of others.
- Theorist. Such individuals prefer to understand the relationships between ideas and are good at creating models that explain how things work.
- Pragmatist. Such individuals prefer to apply and use whatever they have learned in real situations.

5 *Constructivist models.* This approach to learning is essentially based on the view that the 'real' world exists inside the head of

each individual and that it is being constantly modified by largely unconscious mental processes. It essentially provides the personal frame of reference for each individual in understanding life and in the determination of behaviour patterns. From that perspective learning represents a threatening process that might be resisted as it risks challenging the currently held meanings of the world for the individual. So learning based on this approach needs to encourage introspection and reflection in order to integrate the different 'world views' being introduced through the learning process.

6 *Action learning.* This form of learning is achieved through groups seeking to solve real problems, and as a result it introduces interactive and progressive learning into the process. The idea is based on the notion that learning is best linked to real problems that actually require solutions and that any problem can only be partly understood in the early stages. Action learning represents an interactive process involving developing ways of solving the problem by members of a group and then reviewing what actually happens following implementation. Then, as a result of the learning from that experience, more changes are made – and so on.

Training

Traditionally training was regarded as something that shop-floor or lower level employees received in order to allow them to do the work for which they were employed. This was compared to development, which was reserved for senior level employees and managers who were to be developed over the long term as part of their careers. This is now seen as an inappropriate distinction and training is generally regarded as the provision of current job, immediate needs type of development. As such it is frequently referred to as one aspect within an employee development framework.

The starting point for any training or development process is to identify the reason (or need) for it. The need represents a gap of some description and could be identified through any number of ways. It may be that new products or services are to be introduced; a new technology or administrative system is being planned; new ways of working or job changes might have already taken place; or it could be that a new employee needs to be trained to use an existing machine or in the company ways of working. Traditionally, the identification of a training need would be a largely mechanical process involving the need to meet some established requirement. These days, in addition to training being used to meet a job-related need, it might also be used to signal the value that the company places upon employees or the need to facilitate a positive attitude to future change.

Think about it?

Think of examples of how training might be used for developmental purposes.

Development

Development is generally regarded as being less immediate need oriented, longer term and less targeted on specific outcomes. That does not mean to say that development should not have purpose, but it may not be targeted at meeting a particular work-related need in the short term. It is differentiated from training in that it is intended to be supportive of organisational requirements and generally directive of behaviour, but over the longer term. For example, running a leadership development programme for **team leaders** may not be intended to impact in the short term on how the jobholders lead their teams (although aspects of the programme might help in that capacity); it might be intended more to prepare them for appointment to managerial positions. In that capacity it might be a primer as to what to expect in managing a department as compared to leading a team, and a motivator in terms of sending a signal to the group that effective performance in their current role could lead to promotion and career development in the near future.

Learning events

Some of the learning methods used include:

- On-the-job methods. Such as coaching and **mentoring, action learning**, self development, learning logs and contracts.
- Off-the-job methods. In-house, educational and commercially provided courses. Also placements and secondments have a place as part of the development of an individual.
- Open learning, **distance learning** and e-learning methods. These often use electronic or self-study packs which can be used at home or at work, to fit in with working pattern and lifestyle variations.

Evaluating learning

Any learning process should have a purpose otherwise it is simply undirected and wasted effort. The evaluation should be made against what the learning was intended to achieve and that is not always immediate in terms of the impact or specific in terms of outcomes. The usual approach adopted to measuring the effectiveness of any learning event is to measure the impact over several different time periods and across several different measures. For example:

1 *Post-event evaluation.* Collected immediately after a learning event (post-course questionnaire), it seeks to reflect delegate feelings and immediate reaction. The rationale behind this is that if delegates react negatively to an event it probably won't deliver positive benefits to either them or the organisation.

2 *Impact on work behaviour.* This reflects the learning carried back (transferred) to the workplace. This could be assessed by an end of event test of some description if the purpose was to provide delegates with a new skill, or delegates reflecting on what they were able to make use of in their work some time after the event.

3 *Impact on job performance.* This would be measured some time after the end of a learning event and would reflect the degree to which a delegate had been able to apply the learning to their work activities in an enduring way. It could be measured by the delegate reflecting on their performance and/or the line manager undertaking a sort of performance review.

4 *Impact on departmental performance.* This would be measured some time after the event and would be intended to reflect the effect on subsequent work group performance. This level of measure is seeking the line manager perspective on the value for money gained from the use of the training budget. Measures could include efficiency, customer complaints or feedback, cost reduction, quality levels, reduced processing times, and many others. The difficulties with this level of measure are those of time and the effect of many other influencing factors. Many factors contribute to productivity, not just training, making it difficult to identify the cause and effect relationships active in such situations.

5 *Impact on the wider organisational effectiveness.* At this level it is appropriate to seek the views of senior managers (in addition to any tangible evidence) as to the effectiveness of training and development activity in contributing to the achievement of corporate

objectives. In addition to any tangible benefits, there should be a number of less specific effects. For example, greater cooperation between departments might be expected as a consequence or it might be noticed that change becomes less traumatic and easier to achieve.

Think about it?

How might a leadership development programme be evaluated when it was designed for team leaders whose next promotion (in, say, two years' time) would be their first management position?

The learning organisation

The **learning organisation** seeks to have learning deeply embedded in its strategic planning and commercial activities. Mumford (1989) suggests that a learning organisation has several characteristics including:

- Encouragement for managers to identify their own learning needs which should contain challenging goals.
- All employees to have regular feedback on performance and learning.
- Identification of learning opportunities in the design of all jobs and to incorporate into work the opportunity for new experiences from which individuals can learn.
- Encouragement of a questioning attitude to the usual ways of working.
- The acceptance that when learning, some mistakes are inevitable and that they represent a learning opportunity.
- Encouragement of on-the-job training as well as other forms of learning.

Single, double and triple loop learning are ideas that also find expression in the learning organisation. Single loop learning is the process of learning a new skill. It represents the learning achieved from knowing how to select an appropriate choice from a small range of options; it is about efficiency in work activity. The second loop involves the identification of what should be learned. It represents the identification of how to gain effectiveness. The third loop in triple loop learning involves learning in relation to the underlying purpose of the organisation and challenging the status quo during the process. Peter Senge (1990) sought to integrate these ideas into his work in relation to the learning organisation. He identified five disciplines which he claimed could merge into an integrated approach to creating a learning organisation. They are:

1 *Systems thinking.* Understanding the interrelatedness between all aspects of organisational functioning and activity.

2 *Personal mastery.* The need for continuous personal development.

3 *Mental models.* The need to expose the assumptions and gener-alisations involved in the current organisation so that they can be challenged and changed.

4 *Building shared vision.* Shared vision encourages unity of purpose within the organisation.

5 *Team learning.* Based on the view that the capability of the team is greater than that of the individual members hence the need for teams to learn collectively.

Knowledge management

It is difficult to define knowledge other than it being a collective inter-pretation of something and as such constantly open to revision in the light of new knowledge, understandings and experience. It is also very difficult to 'know' how much knowledge is available to an organisation. All organisations have procedures and policies covering much of the activity that takes place, but this can never cover everything that is known or knowable about company activities, its products and services. Equally, it is not possible to 'know' everything that might be known about its actual and potential markets and competitors; or the eco-nomic, political and social environments within which it functions. Some organisations are based around knowledge, consultancies and uni-versities for example. But for all organisations knowledge is increasingly viewed as a critical resource in the battle to survive and prosper in increasingly hostile and ever-changing trading circumstances.

Much of the knowledge within an organisation is carried in the heads of managers and employees and **knowledge management** seeks to capture that expertise in a way that allows it to be shared. The inten-tion is to inform, integrate and use what is known to become a launch-pad for the creation of new understandings and opportunities, for the benefit of individuals and the organisation. Some writers have linked knowledge management with the concept of wisdom – defined in terms of knowledge with a long shelf-life. Lank (2002) suggests that new organisational roles are emerging in an attempt to manage knowl-edge more effectively.

They include:

1 *Knowledge architects.* Senior strategic roles charged with the determination of what knowledge is critical and to be captured; how that should be achieved; how it should be shared; how people will be trained in knowledge management, and how rewarded for collaborative working and knowledge sharing.

2 *Knowledge facilitators.* People with these roles are charged with finding ways of facilitating knowledge flow thorough communication media, indexing and library services, and internal consultancy services.

3 *Knowledge aware people.* These are the users and contributors to the knowledge system.

Think about it?

One definition of knowledge management is 'The management of all knowledge available to the organisation for the benefit of the organisation and the individuals within it.' Martin (2005: 190). Find other definitions and compare them with this one, explaining any differences.

Possible exam and assignment questions. There are many ways in which exam and assignment questions can seek to explore training and development within HRM. The two main ways in which this topic might be found in a question are introduced here. First, as a support theme for the main discussion purpose of the question and secondly, as a theme in its own right. An example of the first type of question might be:

❝Discuss the extent to which effective training and development within a company can assist in its resourcing activities. ❞

The answer to this question would require a discussion of training, development and resourcing, along with a discussion on how they might influence each other. Relevant to that discussion would be issues such as HR planning, retention and resourcing. Training and development is valued by employees as part of their personal career development and future marketability in the increasingly fluid labour market. Therefore, it is likely that a good reputation for training and development would encourage people to seek employment with the company and once employed be more likely to remain for longer periods of time. There are many themes from the material in the appropriate sections that could be integrated into an answer of this type.

An example of the second type of question might be:

❝You have been asked to evaluate the effectiveness of an internal course aimed at improving the people management capabilities of line managers. How would you achieve this objective?❞

The answer to this question would be based on the evaluation of learning events material above. It would be necessary to collect information of various types, including pre- and post-course evaluation scores, perhaps even including interviews with delegates, their superiors and – depending on the nature of the course – trade union representatives. Depending on the number of times the programme has run and over what period of time, it might not be possible to evaluate every level suggested as there may not have been enough time for the effects to filter through to overall company effectiveness. In doing the review it would be neces-sary to identify what was originally intended for the course and what happened subsequently. The results of the review should be presented in the form of a report and circulated to whoever commissioned it.

Textbook Guide

ARMSTRONG: *Chapters 35, 36, 37, 38, 39, 40 and 41.*
BEARDWELL, CLAYDON AND BEARDWELL: *Chapters 8, 9 and 10.*
BLOISI: *Chapter 7.*
FOOT AND HOOK: *Chapters 7 and 8.*
LEOPOLD, HARRIS AND WATSON: *Chapters 12 and 13.*
MARCHINGTON AND WILKINSON: *Chapters 8 and 9.*
PILBEAM AND CORBRIDGE: *Chapter 12.*
REDMAN AND WILKINSON: *Chapters 4 and 11.*
TORRINGTON, HALL AND TAYLOR: *Chapters 17, 18 and 19.*

2.6	
performance management	

The purpose of employing people is to produce something of value to the organisation – as determined by management. Consequently, employees are never totally free to 'do their own thing' and their behaviour must be channelled and controlled if the benefits to management are to be maximised. From the employee perspective, promotion, career development and indeed continued employment depend on being 'defined' as an appropriate performer by managers. This section will explore how these issues are dealt with by HRM specialists.

What is performance?

Performance is one of those words that at first glance seem to be easy to understand and explain. However, as with many areas of human behaviour it is much more complex than is usually imagined. For example, Martin (2005: 429) defines performance as, `The level of achievement by an individual, measured against what they would be expected to achieve.' This implies that the level of achievement can be measured and that it can be compared with what might have been expected. It is easy to 'know' what has been achieved and what could have been achieved if the activity is producing widgets in a factory setting. But what if the activity involves flying an aeroplane, driving a heavy wagon, or teaching HRM to undergraduate students? All three jobs have elements in common, for example schedules to keep and a requirement for the individuals to be able to do the job in the technical and practical sense. But there are other aspects of the jobs that are not so easy to determine in absolute terms. For example, imagine that the aircraft is delayed from taking off at a particular airport because of bad weather, would the late arrival be evidence of poor performance or not? The pilot must make a judgement based on such factors as length of delay, fuel consumption, and passenger safety in deciding an appropriate response to the delay. Does the lecturer hold any responsibility for students who do not pass the HRM module? If so how can this be assessed and what impact should it have on the assessment of their performance?

> **Think about it?**
>
> *How might the performance of a lecturer be assessed? Identify ways in which it might be done and then identify why each 'method' identified might not be appropriate.*

Another issue is who decides what performance means? Usually such decisions are taken by the line managers of the people whose performance is being monitored. It will be up to the **line manager** of the pilot, driver, and lecturer to determine whether or not the performance of their subordinate is acceptable. Many actions in relation to the employment of the individual rest upon such decisions, with pay, training, promotion and continued employment being among the most obvious. Yet for many jobs the experiences of the customer, colleagues or other stakeholders are critical to the relative success of the organisation. Take, for example, a pilot; it is the reaction of passengers to the experience of a particular flight including arrival time, in-flight service, and so on relative to the cost of a ticket that would determine their views about performance. But for individual pilots it is the formal view of their boss that determines their future with the company. Many organisations seek to overcome this difficulty by incorporating multiple perspectives on performance in formal review processes, but the emphasis remains one of performance being 'top-down'.

Compliance versus commitment?

Employers seek to achieve commitment from their employees. Martin (2005: 26) defines commitment as a condition in which, `Employees internalise management's values and norms and in doing so commit themselves to management's aims and objectives.' In effect the employees align with management and their objectives, and in so doing they function automatically and naturally (in their behaviour, attitudes and thinking) in ways preferred by management without having to be directed to do so. It would be clearly beneficial to management if employees were committed as they would be easier and cheaper to manage because of the increased tendency to function automatically in management preferred ways. It also implies that employees would naturally seek to maximise performance in meeting their objectives.

Compliance on the other hand is defined by Martin (2005: 25) as a state in which 'Employees follow the rules precisely, paying only "lip service" to the underlying aims and objectives sought by management.' It might also be added that there can be a tendency for employees to seek to bend or avoid the rules if they can get away with it. Compliance requires the highest levels of input from management as employees must be directed and monitored constantly or they will not deliver what is required of them. Clearly it is not in management's interests to rely on a compliance mode of response from employees – hence the emphasis on achieving commitment.

Of course it is difficult to distinguish between commitment and compliance in practice. In short, just because an employee says that they are committed to the aims and objectives of the organisation it does not mean that they actually are; they may only be complying with an expectation to demonstrate commitment. Many organisations carry out surveys on an annual basis in an attempt to measure commitment, but such 'evidence' does not prove it beyond doubt.

Think about it?

Does the distinction between compliance and commitment matter as long as high performance is being achieved? Why or why not?

Performance management and performance appraisal

There are many issues surrounding performance management including the following:

1 *Management philosophy and style.* The underlying view that management hold about employees as people, their role and value to the organisation, shapes the approach that will be taken to HR policy and practice. The ways in which performance is defined and managed become part of the management approach to the people that they employ. Performance management processes also provide a clear signal to employees about what the company values.

2 *Psychological contract.* The psychological contract reflects the expectations that managers and employees have about their relative rights and responsibilities. That includes the expectations that each party has about what it is reasonable for the employee to contribute in

terms of performance, behaviour, **attitude** and general support in return for the level of 'consideration' received from the employer. In many ways it is the psychological contract that determines the day-to-day activities (including performance) of employees and managers in the work dynamic.

3 *Work organisation and environment.* The way that work is organised – the use of teams, the degree of customer focus to work activities – is just as important to performance as the individual effort, technology, equipment and job design. It has long been assumed that groups encourage individuals to adopt positive behaviour and deliver high performance. However, the opposite effect is not unknown, groups can slow down to the performance of the weakest in order to minimise the level of subsidy to low performers. The management response to poor individual performance (as defined by the group) is a critical determinant of how they will react to such situations.

4 *Clarity and scope of objectives.* The objectives being sought need to be clear and also to reflect the actual purpose of the business if they are to be of any value in directing employee behaviour in terms of performance.

5 *Approach to performance measurement.* There are many examples of performance management schemes which fail because the meaning of performance was not understood. For example, a call centre incentive scheme failed because the company assumed that more calls received would consequently increase sales figures. Operators were paid for the number of calls handled (which increased dramatically) but the calls were not converted into sales. After a few months the scheme had to be withdrawn and replaced by a sales bonus scheme. Many organisations these days seek to use the **balanced business scorecard** as the basis of their performance management approach. It incorporates four different perspectives on corporate performance (financial measures, customer measures, internal business measures, and innovation and learning perspectives) and can be used as the guiding framework for the determination of an integrated performance management process.

Think about it?

Identify other scorecard based approaches that specifically seek to measure the contribution of HR to organisational objectives and strategy.

6 *Motivation to perform.* There are many things that can inhibit the inclination to perform among employees and which can be broadly summarised as the things that disengage them from – or do not effectively connect them to – the objectives being sought. That is not to say that the payment of more money in the form of incentive payments is enough, or even appropriate. One of the difficulties facing managers in the search for effective performance management is that they must inevitably provide support mechanisms at the corporate level (to provide consistency and avoid unfairness or discrimination) but the delivery of 'performance' by the employee remains an individual choice based on daily (or hourly) dynamics involving feelings, attitudes, circumstances, needs, and so on. It is the line managers who must reconcile (through the acting out of the psychological contract) the corporate policy level of performance management requirements with the daily employee behaviour dynamic in order to achieve the 'best' outcome possible.

7 *Reward practices.* This is not just about the level of pay, or the use of financial incentives to perform. It is about the approach to **total reward** (discussed in Section 7 below). The use of financial incentives has a place in performance management but can encourage an **instrumental approach to work**, which in turn can detract from the desire to encourage high levels of commitment. There are a range of non-financial reward possibilities such as praise and reduced control that can encourage individuals to contribute additional performance.

High performance organisations

Many organisations seek to achieve what has become known as high performance working. It can be described as existing in an organisation which displays the following characteristics:

- Sustained market success over time.
- Innovation in quality and customer satisfaction.
- Customer and **continuous improvement** focus.
- Use of self-managed work teams.
- Views the workplace as a source of added value.
- Clear links between training, development and organisational objectives.
- Support for organisational and individual learning.

Performance appraisal

Performance appraisal is part of the performance management cycle. The four stages are:

1 *Identification of job role*. Before performance can be planned it is necessary to understand the role and requirements of the job in question. Ultimately that emerges from the corporate level of planning and objective setting which cascades down to the work group and the identification of job requirements.

2 **Performance planning**. Subsequently, it should be possible to identify what performance means for the jobs in question and to convert it into objectives for a specific review period. Objectives should be SMART (**SMART objectives**) if they are to have any impact, meaning that they should be:

- Specific.
- Measurable.
- Appropriate.
- Relevant.
- Time bounded.

3 *Delivery and monitoring of performance*. It is then for the individual to deliver the expected performance through their day-to-day work activities. The manager retains a monitoring and enabling brief relative to the performance of employees, which might include training, direction, support or interaction with other work groups. During the performance period, it is for the manager to continually review progress (informally) and to seek to encourage the delivery of high performance from the individual.

4 *Formal assessment and reward*. At the end of the performance period there should be a formal review of performance and perhaps the allocation of reward based on the level of achievement as assessed by the manager. There is debate about the value and effectiveness of reward linked to performance based on issues such as the value (and measurability) of targets; the accuracy of manager judgements; the fairness and consistency of judgements; the size of the reward; and the consequences of financially rewarding performance.

Think about it?

Offering a reward linked to performance is paying someone for something that they should be doing as part of their normal work. In practice it indicates that management is incapable of effective leadership; it is a substitute for good management. Critically evaluate this statement?

Performance appraisal – process and perspectives

There are many different types of appraisal process and there are many different perspectives on the performance of individuals including the following.

1 *Performance measures*:

- Measured against specific targets. These might be numbers of units, or delivery of specific outputs.
- Measured against objectives. This could be based on the need to deliver a number of objectives as a department manager. So, for example, deliver a new absence policy, a new incentive scheme and a new age discrimination policy.
- Measured against contributions. It might be that some objectives cannot be delivered as a result of circumstances outside the control of the individual. For example, the CEO may stop a training programme on the basis of cost. But the HR manager may have done a very good job on its justification in relation to business need. It would be unreasonable to regard the non-delivery as a failure of performance in such circumstances. Hence the inclusion of contribution in the process.
- Measured against criteria. This can reflect issues such as attendance, punctuality, dealing with customers, dress code, and so on; the logic being that if such factors are present then performance follows. But just because someone is at work early every day, does not mean that they produce more work of a higher quality.
- Measured against behaviour. It is possible to study what performance means in terms of specific behaviour patterns for each job. The behaviours identified can then be scaled and measured for each employee undertaking that job.

2 *Perspectives on performance assessment*:

- Boss. A top-down view of performance achieved.
- Subordinate. A bottom-up view of the performance of a superior. This is usually done in such a way as to ensure that possible retribution is avoided and that honest opinions are given.
- Peer/colleague. This perspective would be based on the views of people at the same level within the organisation as the job holder (known as **peer appraisal**).
- Customers/suppliers (internal and external). People with whom the individual comes into contact in terms of business processes will also have a view on their performance.
- 360 degree. Seeks to bring together a number of the different perspectives outlined above into a comprehensive, all-round review of the performance of an individual. (see **appraisal-360 degree**)

The design of appraisal forms need to be appropriate to the purpose of the process.

> **Think about it?**
>
> *Someone once described an annual performance appraisal meeting as a, 'dishonest ritual'. Why might that be so and how might such processes be improved?*

Team performance

Research into team working for McKinsey & Company, reported by Kazenbach and Smith (1993) found that a scale of performance related to different types of **team** or group could be identified:

1. *Working group.* A collection of individuals working collaboratively to a limited degree. Performance reflects the efforts of individual members.

2. *Pseudo-team.* Collection of individuals who could achieve higher performance if they became more integrated and effective.

3. *Potential team.* Same as pseudo-teams, but the individuals recognise that they could achieve more.

4. *Real team.* Team committed to a common purpose with appropriate ways of working.

5. *High performance team.* As real teams but also encouraged personal growth and sought to exceed performance expectations among members.

Another feature of **team performance** is the composition of the team in terms of the roles that are necessary for effective decision making to be achieved. There are a number of models (for example, Belbin, 1993) that seek to explain the characteristics associated with the **team roles** that exist.

> **Think about it?**
>
> *Briefly describe the Belbin team roles and provide an explanation of how the model can encourage improved team performance.*

Teams can either be self managed (**autonomous**) or managed, and they engage in different aspects of organisational activity including:

1 *Production and service-related activities.* These are the teams that actually produce the products or services that the organisation sells.

2 *Functional teams.* Such teams are made up of individuals from within the same work or professional group within the organisation. For example, the reward team or maintenance team.

3 *Cross-functional teams.* These teams are made up of individuals from a number of functions and may be charged with achieving a particular objective such as the development of a new product or service.

4 *Problem-solving teams.* These represent a special type of cross-functional or functional team. They are temporary teams created to solve a particular problem and draw in members from a range of appropriate functions. When such a team achieves its objectives it is disbanded.

5 *Management.* Managers have functional responsibilities as well as being involved with new product development, cost reduction, and so on. They are also part of the management team responsible for running the business.

Paying for performance or performance as a reward?

The traditional view was that there existed a natural level of performance that an employee would produce if they were not working under incentive conditions. Therefore, if high performance was required an **incentive scheme** that financially rewarded the individual for producing more than could be naturally expected was needed. This reflects the basic model for all incentive schemes, whether they operate at the factory floor level or among the board of directors. It is argued by some writers that over the last few years the emphasis has shifted to one in which the achievement of high performance should be considered a reward in its own right. This is based on the attempt by managements to create high performance organisations with an emphasis on the individual delivering high performance. Failure to do so by an individual would result in termination of employment or their being allocated low paid menial work.

Possible exam and assignment questions. There are many possible ways in which exam and assignment questions can seek to explore performance management within HRM. The two main ways in which this topic might be found in a question are introduced here: first as a support theme for the main discussion purpose of the question and, secondly, as a theme in its own right. An example of the first type of question might be:

"Discuss the extent to which performance management should be an integral part of the financial reward package offered by an organisation."

The answer to this question would require a discussion of both performance management and reward practice (see Section 7), along with a discussion on how the one might influence the other. There is no right or wrong answer to this question as there are those who believe that performance-related pay should influence financial reward and there are those who do not subscribe to that view. It would be necessary to discuss the basics of performance management and the role of factors such as job design, money, team working and management in achieving high levels of performance. Equally the design of reward (see Section 7) has a part to play in the discussion. It would then be necessary to bring the two parts of the discussion together and offer some conclusions based on the weight of argument and views of the individual answering the question.

An example of the second type of question might be:

"Performance management represents an approach to management control which is dressed up to hide its real intentions and make it more acceptable to employees. Discuss this statement."

The answer to this question would be based on the material summarised in this section of the Companion. The statement implies that effective performance management can make the task of management easier if appropriate employee behaviour, attitudes and support can be assured. Another implication is that it also benefits management through the minimisation of unit labour costs. High performing employees who are committed to the organisation will naturally act in the best interests of management and so fewer problems from conflict and resistance to management's wishes could be expected. Considered from that perspective it would seem that the statement could be supported. However, there is always another side of the argument. It could be suggested that not all managements are manipulative and that crude attempts at manipulation would soon be exposed – leading to conflict, lower performance and other negative conse-quences. There is no right or wrong answer to this type of question. It is neces-sary to explore both sides of the argument and then to propose a reasoned conclusion based on the weight of argument and the views of the individual answering the question.

Textbook Guide

ARMSTRONG: *Chapters 19, 32, 33 and 34.*
BEARDWELL, CLAYDON AND BEARDWELL: *Chapter 6.*
BLOISI: *Chapter 8.*
FOOT AND HOOK: *Chapter 9.*
LEOPOLD, HARRIS AND WATSON: *Chapter 7.*
MARCHINGTON AND WILKINSON: *Chapters 3 and 7.*
PILBEAM AND CORBRIDGE: *Chapter 11.*
REDMAN AND WILKINSON: *Chapters 2, 16 and 19.*
TORRINGTON, HALL AND TAYLOR: *Chapters 11, 12 and 13.*

2.7

remuneration and benefit management

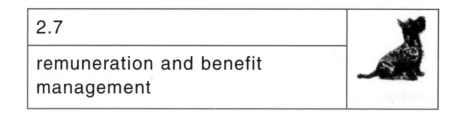

Remuneration management is about finding the most effective basis on which to pay people. Effective in that context usually means the most cost effective consistent with the needs to attract, retain and motivate individuals in a **'felt fair'** manner within the organisation's ability to pay, achieve its strategic objectives and to meet its legal obligations.

Objectives for pay

Both employers and employees have objectives that they seek to achieve through the reward system that they operate under. The key features include those listed in Table 7.1.

Table 7.1

Employer objectives	Employee objectives
1 That pay levels within the company reflect the prestige and status of the organisation	To maximise the purchasing power from the sale of labour by the individual
2 That reward should attract the best people in a competitive labour market	That pay levels are 'felt fair' relative to the scheme and social worth of the job
3 That the reward package should facilitate management control of operational processes	That pay levels are 'felt fair' relative to that of others inside and outside the organisation
4 That reward should encourage high per- formance and motivation	To obtain an appropriate share of wealth created from the work undertaken
5 That reward should not cause labour costs to inhibit commercial activity or success	That pay reflects recognition by the employer for employee contribution
6 That reward should underpin an acceptance of change in behaviour and job activity	That reward should reflect needs and aspirations of employees across their life stages
7 That the outcome from the reward system should be predictable and allow expenditure planning	That the outcome from the reward system should be predictable and allow expendi- ture planning by employees

Elements in a pay structure

Most reward schemes only use a small number of elements from the total range possible. Some of the elements within the reward package may be a contractual requirement (**base pay**) and others may be 'at management's discretion' (some bonus payments). The main elements within a reward package include those listed in Table 7.2.

Table 7.2 Various elements of a reward package

Category	Pay element variations include
Base pay	• No base pay – commission or piecework • Hourly wage • Daily wage • Weekly wage • Monthly salary • Annual salary
Premiums	• Overtime pay • **Shift premium** • Callout payments • Standby payments • Special duties payments • Special responsibility payments • Special conditions payments
Incentive pay	• Productivity bonus payments • Performance related pay • Attendance bonus payments • Additional skill payments • Additional responsibility payments • Profit share and share options
Plussages	• 'Fudge' payments introduced to solve a particular problem and subsequently regarded as 'custom and practice'
Benefits	• Pension • Car/petrol • Holidays • Sick pay • Parental/carer benefits • Training/development/career opportunities • Discounts • Cafeteria benefits

Think about it?

'Felt fair' is an important concept within reward management. With the range of complexity in pay system elements apparent from Table 7.2, can 'felt fair' ever be achieved? If so, how?

Total reward and 'new pay' concepts

The emphasis so far has been on the tangible aspects of the reward package – the **tangible rewards** such as base pay, incentive payments, and **benefits**. These represent the 'total remuneration' level of a reward package. However, that is not the total reward that an employee gains from their job; this includes a broad range of non-financial benefits (also known as non-tangible rewards) that an employee potentially gains such as:

- The experience of carrying out the work itself.
- The atmosphere and positive feelings within the workplace.
- Learning and developmental opportunities available.
- Sense of achievement from knowing that they contribute to the organisation's success.
- Recognition from being a valued member of the organisation.
- Responsibility delegated to the individual.
- Autonomy or freedom of action granted to the individual.
- Growth in personal, job and professional terms as a result of work and organisational design and as a result of the value placed on the individual by management.

The elements included within the total reward concept reflect the **intrinsic rewards** available to enhance the contribution from employees achieved through the financial and extrinsic elements within the package (the **extrinsic rewards**).

New pay recognises the complexity of organisational 'reality' and seeks to shape reward decisions rather than offering specific design principles. It is about seeking ways to use the following principles to enhance strategic effectiveness through reward practice:

- Reward systems should be designed to reward results and behaviour consistent with organisational goals.
- Pay can encourage organisational change.
- A major emphasis on variable pay (pay at risk if results are not delivered).
- Emphasises team as well as individual contribution.
- Employees should have the right to influence the type of reward package adopted.

Strategic reward planning

It is hardly surprising that reward represents a very significant part of the employment relationship. From the employers' point of view there is the inevitable cost associated with the payment of wages and benefits to employees, which for some organisations represents the largest single business cost. Consequently there is a strong pressure to minimise the total cost of labour and also the unit labour cost (a measure of productivity). From the employee perspective the reward package reflects directly on the standard of living and lifestyle of the individual and their family in both the short and the long term (pension is frequently defined as deferred salary); but it also represents a measure of status and success in social terms. The main point to make in this regard is that the reward package holds more significance to both employer and employee than the level of financial reward delivered by it. It holds social and psychological significance for both parties, which adds to the complexity of design and surrounding management issues.

The need to design and manage reward systems is a significant element within the HR planning process, which in turn should be grounded in business strategy. Strategy in general represents a forward looking process intended to guide current and future actions in a defined direction and towards an identified goal. However, as with much HR activity, strategy determination and achievement is never that simple. In the case of HR strategy the key focus is people and their relationship with the employing organisation. People are thinking, active, behaving organisms who can resist, argue, leave, not join in, or display any number of other reactions to the wishes and intentions of others. So changes to HR strategy, particularly in relation to reward management, can be difficult to achieve. The history, traditions and culture of an organisation (together with the industry and location) weigh heavily on any attempt to change future reward policies and practices. In addition the relationship and degree of trust that exists between managers and employees can also impact on any attempt to redesign or introduce changes to a reward system to better align it with business or HR strategy.

Determination of base pay

Base pay means the basic wage paid to an individual in return for them undertaking a particular set of tasks. The decisions around this aspect of reward design include:

1 *Job family structures.* Groups jobs together into 'types' or families (managerial, technical, sales, accounting, and so on) and develops pay structures based on job features and market conditions relevant to each **job family**. Individual family arrangements may be aligned within a common pay framework.

2 *Job evaluation.* Seeks to determine the relative value or size of jobs. There are two types of **job evaluation**: analytical and non-analytical. The **analytical job evaluation** approach seeks to analyse each job (based on a job description) under a number of factors (such as effort, skill and decision making) and award points based on the degree to which each factor is present in the particular job. The larger the number of points awarded to a particular job, the bigger (or greater 'value') it is. **Non-analytical job evaluation** schemes are whole job assessment approaches and do not rely on detailed analysis of the job content. There are three main approaches:

- Job ranking. Sorts the jobs being considered into a rank order from the smallest to the largest.
- **Paired comparisons**. Each job would be compared to each other job and scored as to whether it is superior or inferior to it in terms of its 'value' or 'size'. At the end of the exercise the points for each job would be totalled, with the number of points reflecting the relative size of the job.
- **Job classification**. Starts with a grade structure and appropriate definitions. Then each job is allocated to the relevant grade based on a general interpretation of the nature of the job compared to the grade definition.

3 *Proprietary schemes.* These schemes are designed and sold by consultants who specialise in reward system design. As part of the package they would assist with the implementation and maintenance of the scheme.

4 **Market pricing**. Starts with a job family and seeks to identify the appropriate market rates (through salary or **pay survey**) for that type of work. The information collected could be used to design a **salary structure** for the jobs within the job family.

5 *Competency pay.* Also Known as **competency-based pay**, this is a variation on **skill-based pay**. Pay can reflect the degree of competence that people demonstrate in carrying out their jobs. Additional pay could be earned for the acquisition of new competencies (or skills). This approach encourages people to seek development and places a pressure on managers to find ways of utilising the potential generated. **Competency** requirements can be used as a form of measurement to identify the relative 'size' of jobs.

6 *Grade structures.* Having identified a rank order of jobs then similar jobs need to be grouped together in a grade structure, which in turn would form the basis of a wage structure. This can be a subjective process and care is necessary to avoid discrimination.

7 *Spot rate or wage bands.* **Spot rate pay** means that everyone on a particular grade gets the same wage or salary. **Wage bands** mean that there is a range of pay that is available. If that is the case then some form of pay progression becomes necessary (see below) in order to provide an appropriate process for deciding rates of pay for each individual.

8 *Narrow or broad pay bands.* Narrow bands group jobs together into grades based in small variations in job value. Consequently a large number of grades are created and individuals focus on gaining higher pay by adopting relatively small job changes that will change their grade. **Broadbanding** seeks to reduce the number of wage bands and so encourage a greater emphasis on development and flexibility in work activity as the route to **pay progression**.

Think about it?

To what extent do you think that equality of earnings between men and women can be achieved through the effective use of base pay determination methods?

Pay progression

The use of wage or salary bands means that a range of pay exists for each grade. Consequently it becomes necessary to establish rules for pay progression which determines where an individual will be paid within the range for their grade. There are essentially two options: **incremental progression** and performance progression.

1 *Incremental progression.* Based on the existence of a number of increments or steps from the minimum to the maximum wage level within the grade. Progression to the next increment (unless they are at the top of the scale) could be based either on automatic annual progression or on delivery of an acceptable performance score.

2 *Performance progression.* This is based on there being no incremental steps between the grade minimum and the maximum. Managerial discretion could be used in deciding where an individual should be positioned within the grade, based on their performance and budget constraint. It would also be possible to express the grade in percentage terms, the **midpoint** being 100% and the minimum and maximum being represented as percentages around that midpoint. Rules could then be created that would seek to provide clear guidance

on what performance achievement should produce what wage progression, in percentage position, within the grade. These performance-based reviews may or may not incorporate an annual cost-of-living wage rise into the process.

Pay reviews

Pay levels within a labour market are never static for long. It is essential that market trends are monitored and company reward policy and practice adapted in the light of the information collected. This is usually done through salary or pay surveys carried out on a regular basis. This, together with general economic data and company financial position, allows a general pay policy to be determined – essentially a pay desire. That in turn can be amended by incorporating specific labour market pressures and trends (either upwards or downwards) to create a pay practice position – essentially a pay intention.

Another key element in the pay review process is the role of any trade union or employee representative body in relation to **collective bargaining** over pay and other conditions of work.

Having arrived at the level of pay available for distribution it then becomes necessary to allocate it according to the reward policy rules. That might be to apply cost-of-living rises separately to any performance progression award, or it might incorporate both into a single award through the application of a pay matrix. In the pay matrix there are two factors to be considered: the present position within the grade (measured as a percentage) and the latest performance marking. Using both pieces of information a specific cell is identified within the matrix that would indicate the actual percentage pay award for that individual. In such a scheme the individual 'free-floats' within the pay grade depending upon their performance.

Incentive schemes

There are many thousands of incentive schemes that have been designed over the years. The basic purpose is to encourage people to do more of something than they could reasonably be expected to do. That 'something' could be anything, including a greater volume of output, fewer defects, greater sales levels, higher profits, improvements in share price, and so on. It is about motivating individuals and groups to do more towards achieving the objectives set by the scheme. The relevant decisions include:

1 *Is a scheme appropriate at all?* Incentives are intended to encourage more of something. It implies that there is a known base level of that something and that more could be achieved if people were incentivised. There are a number of major assumptions hidden in that statement. It comes down to a question of what it is reasonable to expect individuals to do in return for the base wage or salary – a very difficult question to answer. It could be argued that managers introduce incentives because they are not capable of achieving the extra something through the application of 'good management' practice. It also allows total wage/salary levels to be disguised for various reasons. For example, a CEO might have a base salary of £100K, but in addition an on-target bonus payment of £150K – bringing total pay to £250K.

Think about it?

What other circumstances might lead to an incentive scheme being introduced for reasons other than to encourage more of something?

---

2 *How should the scheme operate?* Issues that need to be addressed include:

- What type of scheme? – What exactly does more of something mean and how can it be measured?
- Who should be included? – Sales people might be paid commission on sales but what about the support staff who deal with order processing?
- Can the people subject to the scheme actually have an impact on the result? – Everyone in an organisation contributes to the profit levels achieved, but actual profit levels are also subject to economic and competitive forces. What would happen if everyone worked very hard yet profit levels and hence bonus payments were minimal?
- What should the frequency of payment be? – Weekly, monthly, quarterly or annual?
- What should the effect of over or under achievement be on adjacent bonus periods?
- How much will it cost and how complex will it be to administer?
- How easy is it to 'fiddle' the outcome by those subject to the scheme and how can it be prevented?

3 *Group or individual incentive?* Individual incentive schemes often have the most pronounced impact, but tend not to encourage team working. Team incentives can have the opposite tendencies.

4 *How much should the incentive be?* The greater the award possible, the greater the effort to achieve it; but a negative reaction is possible if it is not achieved.

> **Think about it?**
>
> *How might you determine the level of incentive to offer in a sales commission scheme?*

Benefits

The benefit package is intended to support the general well-being of the individual and their family. Such benefits are in addition to the wage of the individual and represent a significant cost for the employer. Not all organisations offer all benefits and some benefits are only available to senior people. The types of benefit available can be categorised under a number if headings such as those listed below.

1 *Personal security:*

- Pension – often referred to as deferred salary.
- Health care – can cover a range of medical, dental and similar provision.
- Insurance – death-in-service, personal accident and business travel.
- Sick pay – perhaps above the legal requirement in terms of level and duration of payment. Possibly also long-term ill-health or incapacity pay.
- Redundancy pay – perhaps above the legal requirement for the loss of a job.

2 *Financial assistance:*

- Mortgage assistance – provides assistance with the cost of buying property.
- Company loans – money loaned at preferential rates of interest for specific purposes.
- Relocation expenses – to assist with the cost of moving home on first appointment or transfer within the company.
- Season ticket loans – low cost loans to cover the cost of buying rail or bus tickets to travel to work.
- Fees to professional bodies – cover the annual fees that may be required (or appropriate) for the employee's work.

3 *Personal needs:*

- Maternity and paternity rights above the legal minimum.
- Leave for personal reasons (paid or unpaid).
- Career counselling – often called outplacement - for people being made redundant.
- Career development and training.
- Team working/well designed jobs.
- Good/effective management practice.

Think about it?

Why might good/effective management practice be classed as a benefit?

- Flexible working – the opportunity to vary the start and finishing times of work.
- Childcare nurseries or vouchers.
- Pre-retirement courses – to prepare people about to retire.
- **Employee assistance programmes** – **counselling** for a wide range of personal and work-related issues or problems including alcohol, drugs, gambling, bullying, stress, and work-related problems.
- Sports and social facilities.
- Discounts on company products.

4 *Holidays* – the right to a specified number of days' holiday each year, along with associated rules on carrying unused days forward and buying or selling days of holiday.

5 *Transport needs:*

- The provision of company cars or a car allowance for those above a certain status or who are required to travel on company business.
- The provision of fuel or mileage allowance to cover the cost of travelling on company business.
- Flight or other travel costs associated with travelling on company business.
- Season ticket loans – low-cost loans to cover the cost of buying rail or bus season tickets to travel to work.

6 **Affinity benefits** – these cover a range of possible benefits (such as reduced price medical cover, insurance, retail discounts and so on) that are provided by a third party and which the employer offers to employees at a special price.

Many organisations offer **cafeteria or flexible benefit** schemes within the total reward approach. Benefit packages are expensive and research has shown that not all employees value (or need) all of the benefits available to them. Consequently, reward specialists get more value from the benefits used by the organisation through flexible distribution, which involves allowing employees to select a particular mix of benefits appropriate to their needs from a defined range available. The idea here is to reduce the cost of providing benefits, match the benefits taken up by an employee with their needs, and to play a positive role in employee motivation and retention by achieving greater impact from the benefit part of the reward package.

Possible exam and assignment questions. There are many possible ways in which exam and assignment questions can seek to explore reward management within HRM. The two main ways in which this topic might be found in a question are introduced here: first as a support theme for the main discussion purpose of the question, and secondly, as a theme in its own right. An example of the first type of question might be:

"Discuss the extent to which the financial reward package offered by an organisation can be used effectively within a resourcing programme."

The answer to this question would require a discussion of both reward practice and resourcing along with a discussion on how the one might influence the other. In essence there is no right or wrong answer to this type of question as there are organisations who firmly believe that paying the highest wage or salary automatically attracts the best candidates and there are organisations which prefer to attract candidates on the basis of the non-financial elements within the total reward concept. It would be necessary to bring the two aspects of the discussion together and offer some conclusions based on the weight of argument and views of the individual answering the question.

An example of the second type of question might be:

"The introduction of any incentive scheme is an admission by management that it cannot provide effective leadership within the organisation. Discuss this statement."

The statement is making the points that it is very difficult to know what should be expected as a fair day's work for a fair day's pay and that good leaders have the ability to get more commitment and 'deliverables' from subordinates than ineffective leaders. The question asks that the student takes a view in relation to that point and argues their case. It would be possible to agree with the statement, but in doing so it would be necessary to show how an incentive scheme can be a leadership substitute. Equally, it would be possible to argue against the statement by arguing that used appropriately incentives can achieve things that might not otherwise be possible. In addition there is the political and employee relations dimension – some incentive schemes are not classed as part of the pay package for pension or other purposes and so the company can pay more without adding significantly to its overall labour cost. There is no right or wrong answer to this type of question. It is necessary to explore the arguments and then to propose a reasoned conclusion based on the weight of argument and the views of the individual answering the question.

Textbook Guide

ARMSTRONG: *Chapters 42, 43, 44, 45, 46, 47, 48 and 49.*
BEARDWELL, CLAYDON AND BEARDWELL: *Chapter 6.*
BLOISI: *Chapter 6.*
FOOT AND HOOK: *Chapter 10.*
LEOPOLD, HARRIS AND WATSON: *Chapter 8.*
MARCHINGTON AND WILKINSON: *Chapter 12.*
PILBEAM AND CORBRIDGE: *Chapters 9 and 10.*
REDMAN AND WILKINSON: *Chapter 5.*
TORRINGTON, HALL AND TAYLOR: *Chapters 27, 28 and 29.*

2.8	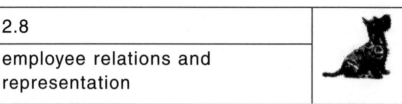
employee relations and representation	

Employee relations

Employee relations can be defined as the management of the employment relationship. That might seem a simplistic explanation of the term but it carries with it a broad range of implications. It is more than deciding the terms of the employment contract, or of the salary review. It is about every aspect of the organisation and how it impacts on the management of people and the creation of a high performance work environment.

Until recently employee relations took as 'given' that union membership was the norm among employees and that it generally involved collective bargaining. However, with the almost continual decline in trade union membership since the late 1970s these views have, of necessity, been brought into question. See Table 8.1 for comparative figures for union membership.

Table 8.1

Year	Trade union membership	Percentage of total workforce (%)
1979	13 million	58
2002	7.3 million	26.6

The reasons for the decline in trade union membership are many and varied including:

1 *Anti-trade union legislations.* Introduced during the 1980s, this made it more difficult for unions to organise **industrial action** and **strikes** and also made it impossible to maintain pre-entry closed shops (membership of a specific union a requirement before employment could be offered).

2 *Industrial restructuring.* A decline in traditional industries in which union membership was the norm and the growth of industries with traditionally low levels of union membership. The growth industries were difficult for the unions to organise recruitment in (call centres, hospitality, tourism and retailing for example). The average size of workplace has also reduced making it more difficult to recruit union members.

3 *Economic factors.* With the growth in the economy it is comparatively easy for individuals to move jobs rather than have to stay and fight for changes to conditions of work.

4 *Social factors.* People are more prepared to take responsibility for their own **career progression**, income, development and work patterns. Consequently they will change job if their needs are not met by the current employer.

5 *Ability of unions to influence employers.* During the 1980s it became very difficult for the unions to have any influence over job losses, business reorganisations, organisational relocations and demands for productivity improvement. Consequently union members began to question the value of membership.

6 *Organisational culture and attitudes.* As a result of the above changes employers have had to develop new ways of managing employee relations in order to attract, retain and motivate employees without relying on collective bargaining agreements. There is now much greater emphasis on the individual, rewarding/encouraging high performance and of creating the conditions that generate commitment, trust and loyalty between managers and employees.

The question remaining is whether or not trade union membership levels will remain low and continue to decline, or whether they will once again grow to become a dominant force in HRM policy and practice? Only history will be able to answer that question with any certainty but signs are contradictory and suggest either growth or further decline in membership. Membership levels among the under-30 age group declined between 1990 and 2000 and the fastest growing job opportunities are in those areas with traditionally low membership rates. The opposite view is based on the fact that the trade unions have been through periods of steep decline in membership levels in the past and have gone on to recover and increase membership as employment conditions have changed. Survey research has also shown that people (including the young) who are not currently trade union members are not hostile towards, or opposed to joining, they simply don't have the opportunity or see the benefit.

Think about it?

Has the level of trade union membership declined in the public sector to the same extent as in the private sector? Why or why not?

Forms of representation and employee representative bodies

In the UK trade unions tend to be occupationally based, for example there is a trade union that represents journalists. There also exists a wide range of organisationally based employee representative bodies that may or may not meet the legal requirements of being a trade union or be registered as one. Such employee associations provide employees of the organisation with a common voice and collective support when dealing with management and may, in practice, function as a local trade union. The major disadvantage of such bodies is that unless they exist in very large organisations and charge a membership fee they will be unlikely to have access to any resources other than can be provided on a voluntary or part-time basis, or provided by management. As a consequence there is, inevitably, some doubt about the degree to which they can act independently of management in representing the interests of employees.

Think about it?

How might you define a trade union?

Recognising unions to represent the interests of employees signifies a fundamental change to the way in which management functions in relation to its treatment of people. Imagine a snapshot of an organisation. This picture represents the organisation as a collection of groups – all with differing interests, but with an overarching 'common purpose' and 'unity' holding them together. Once an external body (union) is introduced into that context the analogy no longer holds and the picture describes a family with the divorce lawyer and police already in attendance to deal with the warring parties!

Think about it?

Under what circumstances might a negative view of a trade union be created within an organisation? How might that situation be changed?

There are many possible responses to a request from a trade union for **recognition** as the employee representative body within an organisation. They include:

1 *Ignore the issue.* This reaction is based on a hope that by ignoring the approach the trade union will give up and withdraw from any interest in seeking recognition.

2 *Delaying tactics.* This is based on the view that recognition will probably be inevitable, but that it should be done on management's

terms. The tactic is about buying time to 'put the house in order' and might involve raising wage levels; improving conditions of work; changing the management style; employing an HR specialist; and so on.

3 *Enter into discussions.* This could result in a number of outcomes, including:

- Refusal to recognise. The employer refuses to discuss any employee matter with the trade union.
- Agreement to individual representation. This results in an agreement that allows the union to represent an individual subject to disciplinary action or who was pursuing a grievance. However, there are legislative rights that 'recognised' unions have that would take precedence.
- Agreement to representation and **consultation**. In addition to individual rights the agreement would allow for the union to be consulted over a range of employee relations issues. Legal rights also impact on the ability to limit representation to these areas.
- Agreement to representation, consultation and collective bargaining. Seeks either to embrace the union as a stakeholder or to prescribe in specific detail the boundaries of the relationship, and the rights and responsibilities of both parties. In addition to the other rights the union has the opportunity to negotiate with management on terms and conditions of employment on behalf of specified employees.

In addition to the content of recognition there are options for deciding on the range of unions that might be recognised:

- **Multi-union recognition**. This means more than one union within the company, each recognised for a specific category of employees (factory, staff, maintenance, and so on) and with different recognition agreements in place. Separate negotiations would be held with each union.
- **Single-union recognition**. The company recognises one union for all categories of employee.
- **Single-table bargaining**. Multiple unions are recognised within a particular company, each with a separate recognition agreement, but each with a clause making provision for common negotiations. For this to work the trade unions must be willing and able to work together.

There is also the possibility for derecognition of a union – where the company terminates an existing agreement. It may arise for any of the following reasons:

- Management have decided to adopt a 'macho' approach to employee relations.
- The level of membership in the union falls to an unsustainable level, thus making recognition impractical.
- A planned change to recognition, perhaps moving to a single-union agreement.

> **Think about it?**
>
> Draw up an argument supporting trade union recognition and then create an argument for the benefits of derecognition. Which is the most convincing argument and why?

Trade unions and the law

A complex legal framework exists for trade unions seeking recognition within an organisation. In brief, a union can seek recognition to be forced on an unwilling employer through the **Central Arbitration Committee (CAC)**. The CAC can (when more than 20 people are employed) encourage a voluntary agreement between the company and the trade union. Failing that, the CAC can pursue either of the following courses:

1. *Require management to recognise the trade union* (where over 50 per cent of employees within the proposed bargaining group are already members), unless it can be shown that sufficient members do not wish the union to be recognised, or the CAC can be persuaded that it would not be in the interests of good employee relations.

2. *Organise a ballot of the workforce* within the proposed bargaining group to determine the level of support for recognition. To succeed the result must achieve a positive response from a majority of those voting and at least 40 per cent of those eligible to vote.

In the UK collective agreements are not usually legally binding and are binding 'in honour only'. An exception exists in the case of recognition awarded by the CAC, when a failure to abide by the decision can result in legal action against the employer.

Other rights conferred on trade unions as a result of legislation include:

- Consultation over redundancy plans involving 20 or more people.
- Consultation over a transfer of business undertakings between employers.
- Consultation over health and safety matters.
- Consultation over pensions where the employer scheme would be 'contracted out' of the State Earnings Related Pension Scheme.
- Right to be involved in the European Works Councils for any business operating on that scale. Also to be informed and consulted about plans and issues in relation to their employment as a result of the EU directive extending the original rights (as moderated by the UK government).

- Consultation over workplace agreements covering the Working Time Regulations, maternity and paternity rights.
- Individual representation covering representation at disciplinary hearings, whether or not the union is formally recognised by the employer or not.

Employee involvement and empowerment

Employees are automatically involved with the organisation to a significant degree because their financial wellbeing and career is dependant on the success of it. However, **employee involvement** is usually taken to mean more than a passive interest in the running of an organisation. It refers to a direct involvement in the decision making of the business in a way that would traditionally be regarded as the preserve of management. The opportunity to have employee representatives directly involved in the running of a business is enshrined in European law through the requirements to set up European Works Councils for relevant organisations from 2001, and under the more recent directives extending information and consultation rights (modified by the UK government).

Employee empowerment refers to a delegated responsibility to take decisions without reference to higher authority. The individual is given greater decision-making responsibility than their job function would usually permit. It is an attempt to overcome slow decision making; reduce the levels of management required; improve customer service; and maximise employee engagement with the business.

Among the involvement and empowerment practices that can be found in originations are the following:

1 *Information sharing and downward communication.* Based on the need to share information so that it can be used effectively to support business objectives.

2 *Upward problem solving.* Representative participation (not everyone is directly involved) is one way of getting more people involved in decision making. Having everyone involved in initiatives such as **quality circles**, team/department meetings, and having employee members on other company committees allows the maximum number of people to get involved in decision making.

3 **Financial participation**. Involves giving employees a financial stake in the success of the business. Profit share and share option schemes are the most common forms of this type of involvement.

4 *Task autonomy.* Represents delegated responsibility for a discrete part of the work of the business. For example, a team might

be given the responsibility for accounts payable and as such be allowed to decide for itself how the work should be done and how it should be allocated between members of the team.

5 *Attitudinal encouragement.* Involves providing the necessary training, support and encouragement to absorb the values, behaviours and standards determined by management as appropriate to the effective running of the business. One writer (Taylor, 1998: 98) has suggested that in the service sector where competition is particularly aggressive, employers equate this approach with requiring customer facing staff to 'deep act' to provide the strongest possible connection with customers and their needs.

6 *Self management.* The individual or team are allowed to self manage in a deliberate attempt to flatten the organisational structure and empower employees.

7 **Total Quality Management (TQM).** This is superficially about quality improvement. However, in order to maximise quality it is necessary to deal with every element of organisational activity that hinders its achievement. It requires the involvement and participation of everyone in finding how every tomorrow can be better than every today.

Think about it?

Assess the argument that employees already put their well-being at risk by working for a company (their income is dependant on it) and that financial participation simply increases their level of risk for no real benefit?

Forms of industrial action

There are many possible forms of industrial action that are available to both employees and managers. The most common are:

1 *Strike.* A withdrawal of labour by employees. There are legal requirements covering the need to ballot members before such action can be sanctioned and about the use of secondary pickets. The aim of a strike is to bring the organisation to a standstill and so force the employer to negotiate and to concede more of the union's demands. There are various forms of strike ranging from the protracted withdrawal of labour to the short one or two days of action at

intervals timed to cause maximum disruption to company operations with minimal loss of earnings to employees.

2 **Lockout**. The opposite of a strike in that management refuse to allow workers to enter company premises or to work.

3 **Work to rule**. Involves following the established rules and procedures to the letter, with no exceptions. In a perfect world this should have no effect on the normal running of a business, but it invariably does. The reasons for that include:

- Procedures and rules become outdated over time and do not reflect current operating practice.
- The range of goods and services offered by the organisation and customer requirements change, with procedures failing to keep up.
- Exceptions to the rules occur creating precedents that then become the norm. Few procedures and rule frameworks cover every eventuality.
- Organisations function in a dynamic environment and things occur requiring 'ways' around problems to be found. These become the norm but procedures and rules may not be updated.
- Most of the time 'things' work because people make them do so; procedures and rules can easily drift away from being relevant.
- Keeping procedures and rules up to date is expensive and takes time and so gets pushed to the back when organisation are under pressure.
- Human nature is inventive and people find 'short-cuts' to doing their jobs as a way of making work easier, saving time, increasing bonus earnings, meeting targets, making work interesting, and so on – all of which mean that the rules and procedures get 'bent' over time.
- Rules and procedures are sometimes developed on the basis of ensuring that the risk of litigation or prosecution is minimised rather than for operational guidance. Therefore the opportunity is created to follow procedure and disrupt routine activity.

4 **Go slow**. This simply means doing less work than would usually be the case. Claiming payment while not actually doing anything would make the employee liable for disciplinary action. But what is a reasonable level of work? Financial incentives encourage higher productivity (compared to what might be expected) and an employee might reasonably take a view that they do not want the additional money and so 'take it easy'. It is the ambiguity that creates the opportunity for industrial action.

5 *Overtime/flexibility restriction*. Refusing to work (or offer) overtime or to work flexibly when that has been the norm can quickly impact on the organisation's ability to meet customer needs.

6 *Withdraw of good will.* Not co-operating enthusiastically with management expectations about the normal running of the company. Failing to pass messages quickly or to simply lose enthusiasm when dealing with customers can have a significant impact on company operations.

It might be apparent from the foregoing discussion that management have fewer levers in relation to industrial action than employees. That, along with the need to maximise employee commitment and contribution to the organisation, is why employee relations is an important aspect of HR.

Think about it?

Should industrial action be illegal under all or any circumstance? Why or why not?

Negotiating in employee relations

Negotiation can be defined as 'a process of forming agreements between individuals and groups who have mutually dependant needs and desires' (Martin, 2005: 671). It is about establishing the basis and boundaries of a relationship and about resolving difficulties that have arisen during the execution of an agreement. There are many approaches to negotiation as a process and there are five basic approaches to dealing with problems as they occur:

- Avoid – ignore the issue and hope that it will go away.
- Smooth – calm the situation without really giving anything away or dealing with the underlying problem, that is, 'put-it-off'.
- Force – about the application of brute force and pressure in any way that will cow the other side into submission, this is the bullying or macho approach to management. Leads to a 'win-lose' approach to negotiation – every point conceded is a loss to that side.
- Compromise – splitting the difference in trying to give all parties something of what they asked for.
- Confront – identify and face up to the underlying problem and then find ways of solving it. Seeks to understand the full nature of the problem and the viewpoints of all parties and only then seeking ways of achieving mutual benefit in the solution.

One approach to negotiation is the four step **'Principled Negotiation'** model developed by Fisher and Ury (1986):

1 *Separate the people from the problem.* Ignoring personal likes and dislikes and focussing on the issue draws attention to finding good solutions.

2 *Focus on interests, not positions.* Negotiations usually start with each party stating its opening position. These are not necessarily the underlying interests that each will have. Identifying the underlying interests that each party holds prepares the ground for the next step in the model.

3 *Invent options for mutual gain.* This is the creative part within the model and requires the parties to actively seek to solve the problems in ways which provide mutual benefit.

4 *Insist on objective criteria.* How to decide when a deal is a good deal and how its success (or failure) should be measured – avoid conjecture, guesswork and vague expressions of outcomes.

Think about it?

To what extent might it be possible to eliminate negotiation in employee relations? Why?

Possible exam and assignment questions. There are many possible ways in which exam and assignment questions can seek to explore employee relations and representation within HRM. The two main ways in which this topic might be found in a question are introduced here: first as a support theme for the main discussion purpose of the question and, secondly, as a theme in its own right. An example of the first type of question might be:

❝Discuss the extent to which reward management is the only significant aspect of employee relations these days and then only in organisations which recognise trade unions.❞

The answer to this question would require a discussion of both reward management and employee relations, along with a discussion of the significance of one for the other. There are other aspects of work such as commitment, attitude change and employee empowerment that would also have relevance to this discussion. There are those who believe that negotiation with employees or unions has no relevance in modern management and who focus on individuals to maximise their contribution. Equally there are those who believe in partnership arrangements, and who seek to move forward with the informed consent and agreement of all employees and their representatives. For a good answer it would be necessary to bring the various aspects of the discussion together, offering some conclusions based on the weight of argument and views of the individual answering the question.

An example of the second type of question might be:

"It should be possible to eliminate negotiation from management-worker relations if both parties work honestly with each other. Discuss this statement."

The statement is making the point that it should be possible to eliminate negotiation from employee relations. This has been tried without much success. It left no scope for employee representatives to shape or influence the management intention, leaving them with no effective role. Such an approach might place employees more firmly under management control and give them no freedom of action or choice in the matter. This could lead to frustration and anger as a result. So even though logic suggests that with honesty and openness on both sides leading to greater levels of trust then negotiation should be unnecessary, it seems to be a necessary part of the human experience of work. For a good mark it would be necessary to explore both sides of the argument, and then to propose a reasoned conclusion based on the weight of argument and the views of the individual answering the question.

Textbook Guide

ARMSTRONG: *Chapters 50, 51, 52, 53 and 54.*
BEARDWELL, CLAYDON AND BEARDWELL: *Chapters 11 and 13.*
BLOISI: *Chapter 9.*
FOOT AND HOOK: *Chapter 13.*
LEOPOLD, HARRIS AND WATSON: *Chapter 15.*
MARCHINGTON AND WILKINSON: *Chapters 10 and 11.*
PILBEAM AND CORBRIDGE: *Chapters 15 and 16.*
REDMAN AND WILKINSON: *Chapters 7 and 15.*
TORRINGTON, HALL AND TAYLOR: *Chapter 21.*

2.9	
discipline and grievance handling	

In the modern world, management must function by consent to a much greater degree than has been possible historically. Individuals have to be persuaded to comply with management intentions to a much greater degree than was the case. That does not mean that managers do not set (or apply) the rules under which employees operate, but their actions are much more likely to suffer scrutiny than would have formerly been the case. If managers cannot rely on an automatic and unquestioning compliance with their wishes then they must find alternative ways of harnessing employee effort into a collective endeavour that supports the objectives sought.

Think about it?

How might managers ensure that employees contribute effectively to organisational goals when they must rely heavily on consent rather than the right to obedience in directing employee effort?

Power, control or organisational justice?

One view holds that in an organisational context the threat of disciplinary action is how managers seek to exercise power and control over employee behaviour. The existence of a grievance process is viewed as the way that employees respond to management actions if they feel that the application of power and control has become too aggressive.

Another view is that discipline and grievance is about achieving **organisational justice**. The employment relationship is based on the existence of a contract which sets out the rights and responsibilities of both parties. If either party becomes dissatisfied with the behaviour of the other in relation to the contract then an organisational mechanism exists to address that concern. For the employer the disciplinary procedure provides the means of raising any 'problems' with the individual.

By doing so it should be possible to identify the underlying reasons for the 'problems' and find ways of overcoming them one way or another. Equally, if the employee is unhappy with some of the employer's actions the grievance procedure provides the opportunity to raise the issue formally and so have it dealt with. Of course raising either discipline or grievance issues does not guarantee satisfaction for the individual (or manager) raising them. However they provide formalised mechanisms through which organisational justice can be aimed at.

Think about it?

To what extent is the notion of 'organisational justice' an attempt to disguise the power and control aspects of management?

Discipline in practice

In its broadest organisational sense discipline is about the direction of human behaviour in order to produce a controlled performance. Organisations consist of many people who must all work together to allow the products and services to be delivered to the customer in a planned and controlled way. It is the job of management to capture and channel human endeavour in pursuit of planned and controlled activity so that business objectives can be achieved in a timely and cost-effective manner. In practice much management endeavour is focused on the desire to minimise the variability in human behaviour. Such an approach is the basis of the management-by-exception approach to the task, in which any variation in expected activity or behaviour would be investigated and appropriate action identified.

Discipline is about the control of human behaviour and as such there are many approaches to achieving it including:

- Resourcing. The recruitment of people who fit with the ethos of the company, work colleagues and the type of work.
- Induction. A way of easing the individual into the organisation in such a way that they acquire the necessary norms of behaviour and attitude.
- Training. Presents a wide range of behaviour control opportunities. For example, selection for training sends a signal – either 'punishment' (remedial training) or 'developmental' (someone worth investing in). During training an opportunity exists to reinforce management messages about behaviour and attitudes.

- Culture. Management actively seek to develop appropriate cultures that will help to shape appropriate employee behaviours.
- Rules. Rules are a requirement to behave in specified ways and so they shape employee behaviour. Knowing that the rules will be enforced also encourages compliance.
- Management style. A dictatorial style may encourage behaviours that superficially comply with management intentions or actively undermine them.
- Expectations. The expectations that management have in relation to employee behaviour will influence what actually happens.
- Delegated responsibility. If everything has to be passed upwards or to another person for approval it creates a 'couldn't-care-less' attitude.
- Job design. Can allow the individual to develop a commitment to the achievement of management's objectives.
- **Team work**. Team working pressures individuals to conform to the norms of team behaviour. Appropriate behaviour norms that support management intentions are needed; if not, actual behaviour patterns can subvert the intentions.

Looked at in its broadest sense the organisational approach to discipline (in the sense of the delivery of appropriate and controlled behaviours as expected by management) can be regarded as a series of levels:

1 *Managerial discipline.* Is about managers giving clear direction about what should be done, when and how. It is what might be experienced when first joining a company.

2 *Team discipline.* This occurs in a work group and is based on the mutual need of the team members to present a united front in keeping the team together and achieving the objectives set. It requires a lower level of direct input from management to direct behaviour.

3 *Self discipline.* This represents the highest level of discipline and exists where an individual takes responsibility for their own actions and behaviours. It is all about self-control and taking responsibility for personal actions. At this level of discipline, very little direct management intervention or direction would be required. It does, however, require trust to exist between management and the employee.

Grievance in practice

Grievance relates to something that makes an individual feel oppressed in some way or other. There are different levels of severity for such events:

1 *Dissatisfaction.* This level represents something that disturbs the individual, resulting in a feeling of disquiet. It is unlikely to lead to the individual externalising the problem or its effect on them.

2 *Complaint.* This level represents something more significant in its effect as it results in the individual externalising the problem by talking or grumbling to others in an informal way.

3 *Grievance.* This level represents a more significant event in that the individual feels the need to formally present the complaint to management so that it is properly addressed. It invariably involves using the grievance procedure available within the company.

There are different types of complaint that can arise and they can be generalised into three categories:

1 *Factual.* This type of complaint is based on something (a fact) that can easily be checked and dealt with.

2 *Subjective reactions.* This type of complaint is slightly more diffi-cult to deal with as the effect will be different for each person. For example, someone might complain that it 'is too hot to work in this room'. This may be true for them but will not necessarily apply to every other person. The difficulty for the person receiving the com-plaint is to find a way of responding without creating complaints from people not affected by the original problem.

3 *Hopes and fears.* This type of complaint represents the most dif-ficult to deal with as the 'problem' as presented may not be the real cause for the grievance. For example, an individual who com-plains that their manager has favourites might actually be worried about job security. Their line of thinking might be: 'When asked to work overtime in the past I have always refused as I have a lot of outside interests and commitments. My manager no longer asks me to work overtime as she knows that I would refuse. However, I have now heard that job cuts are likely and that performance might be the deciding factor for who is selected to be made redundant. I am wor-ried that my refusal to work overtime might count against me in this selection process'. Complaints based on hopes and fears are very difficult to detect as they often appear as one of the other cate-gories. To detect them it is necessary for the manager dealing with the issue to carefully ask questions in an attempt to get at the feel-ings, attitudes and thoughts behind the problem as stated.

> **Think about it?**
>
> *How (if at all) could you deal with a problem as described in point 3 above if it were presented to you as a manager?*

Company discipline procedures

In essence there are two possible approaches to discipline within an organisation, they are informal and formal.

Informal approaches to discipline

Informal approaches to discipline can cover many interventions ranging from guidance or instruction to an employee from a supervisor to perform a particular task in a particular way or at a particular time, to a telling off given to an employee by a supervisor or manager for doing something wrong, not working as they should be or making a mistake. Such a telling off may be done publicly or privately, in the manager's office.

Most discipline takes place within normal interaction between superiors and subordinates (or even between colleagues). As such it is not regarded as a significant event and is part of the normal supervisory process. However, informality can lead to problems if the employee becomes subject to frequent admonishment. It is not uncommon for a manager to want to dismiss an employee after several informal warnings without the formal procedure ever having been followed. Consequently, there exists a fine line between the informal approach to managing people at work and the need to ensure that formal procedures are used when appropriate.

Formal approaches to discipline

There are usually a number of stages or steps in a formal company discipline procedure. They are:

1. *Verbal warning.* This would be applied to situations involving minor episodes of misconduct. Although classed as a verbal warning it should be recorded in writing, and a copy given to the employee. The

document should summarise the 'problem'; set out what the employee is required to do and by when; identify what support will be provided by management during the process; and also what will happen if repeated occurrences of the 'problem' arise. Review meetings should also be included in the outcome to monitor and encourage employee progress in meeting the stated requirements.

2 *Written warning.* This might be used for repeated occurrences of minor misconduct (where the verbal warning has not changed the employee behaviour) or for events more serious than would warrant a verbal warning. The written warning given to the employee (and kept on file) should be identical in format and content to that described under verbal warning. Review meetings should also be included in the outcome to monitor and encourage employee progress in meeting the stated requirements.

3 *Final written warning.* This level is either used when the behaviour expected as the outcome from a written warning does not materialise, or when an event occurs that is so significant that it is almost serious enough to justify dismissal. The final written warning document given to the employee (and kept on file) should be identical in format and content to that described under verbal warning. Review meetings should also be included in the outcome to monitor and encourage employee progress in meeting the stated requirements.

4 *Dismissal.* This stage would arise when the requirements of the final written warning have not been met or when a serious event occurs, the most serious occurrences of which would be referred to as **gross misconduct**. Dismissal for gross misconduct means that the individual's employment is terminated without the contractual right to notice under the contract of employment. It represents a category of misconduct which is so serious that it allows the employer to dismiss the employee without giving them the opportunity to redeem themselves. As an alternative to dismissal some procedures allow for disciplinary transfer, demotion or **suspension** without pay, but these should only be used if appropriate contractual provision exists.

In addition to the procedural steps, other requirements must be taken into account, such as the need for:

- Reasonable investigation processes to identify the 'facts' associated with the case. This may involve interviews, taking statements, and in some circumstances suspension (with pay) of the person during the investigation.

- Reasonable hearings so that the case can be fully explored and the individual given the chance to put their side of the story and challenge the evidence.
- Allowing representation from a trade union representative or a colleague.
- Reasonable timescales. Hearings should be held within a reasonable and stated timescale. The right of appeal should also be exercised within a specified reasonable time, as should the period during which disciplinary action stays 'live' on an employee's file.

Think about it?

What does the term 'length of time that a warning stays live' mean and what are its implications in relation to disciplinary action taken against an employee?

- A right of appeal against the decision to a higher authority not previously involved in the case.
- Limits on authority. Not every manager has the right to dismiss an employee and so the procedure needs to indicate the level of management authorised to do so.

Company grievance procedures

Grievance procedures usually contain a number of stages. For example, the stages might be as follows:

1 *Informal hearing.* The individual would be expected to present the grievance informally (in writing) to their immediate manager. A meeting to discuss the 'problem' would be arranged within a reasonable timescale and the issues explored. An outcome should then be made known to the employee within a specified timescale.

2 *Formal hearing.* If the matter is not satisfactorily resolved then the individual would raise the grievance (in writing) with a more senior manager. A meeting to discuss the 'problem' would be arranged within a reasonable timescale and the issues explored. An outcome should then be made known to the employee within a specified timescale.

3 *Appeal.* If the matter is not satisfactorily resolved at the previous stage then the individual would have the right of appeal to a more

senior manager for one last review. In some cases there might exist a review panel involving joint management and union members, or alternatively an external arbitration process.

If the grievance is a collective problem (affecting a number of people) then it is possible that a separate disputes procedure exists allowing a trade union to represent the employee case to management along with the right of appeal to some form of external conciliation or arbitration process.

Legal aspects

There are a number of legal rights associated with discipline and grievance within organisations. In disciplinary situations the main legal dimension is the right to raise a claim of **unfair dismissal** if the employee considers that their employment has been terminated unfairly. The law requires that any dismissal should be based on a reasonable belief (of guilt) following a reasonable investigation and a fair hearing carried out within the provision of an appropriate procedure (or in the absence of a company procedure the application of the statutory procedure). The law makes provision for a dismissal to be fair if it falls into one or more of the following categories:

- Redundancy.
- Legal bar.
- Capability.
- Conduct.
- Retirement.
- Some other substantial reason (SOSR).

Where an individual feels that they have been unfairly dismissed they could make application (within three months of the effective date of termination) to an Employment Tribunal outlining the basis of their case. A copy of the claim would be sent to the former employer who would be asked to respond within a specified timescale. The response would be sent to the applicant and a date set for a tribunal hearing. Copies of all of the paperwork would also be sent to the Advisory, Conciliation and Arbitration Service (ACAS) who would seek to resolve the matter without the need for a tribunal hearing. Should that not prove possible then the tribunal would meet and hear the case, and make its award either in favour of the applicant or the employer. If the dismissal was found to have been unfair then the tribunal will make an award, which can be:

1 *Reinstatement.* The employer is ordered to take the employee back into the same job and on the same terms of employment and with no loss of service. If the employer refuses then the tribunal can award additional compensation.

2 *Re-engagement.* To take effect after the hearing, but with no continuity of service.

3 *Compensation.* This represents a financial award to compensate for the loss of the job. There are rules covering how the award is calculated, based on service, job prospects and the employee's contribution to their dismissal.

Think about it?

Find out the current rules and level of compensation applied by a tribunal once it has made a finding of unfair dismissal.

Either or both parties can opt to be represented by a legal representative, trade union officer or other person during tribunal hearings. The tribunal is comprised of three people: a legally qualified chair, and two lay side-members – one drawn from an employers' nominated list of suitable candidates and the other from an equivalent trade union nominated list. In certain circumstances it is possible for the losing side to appeal against the findings of a tribunal to the Employment Appeal Tribunal (EAT) and potentially beyond that to the other superior courts within the judicial system.

It would be possible for an individual to raise a grievance, have it rejected by the employer, and then to resign and claim that they had been constructively dismissed. By so doing they would have the opportunity to seek redress for **constructive dismissal** before an Employment Tribunal. In most cases, however, this would not be possible. There are cases of discrimination and other events at work which do allow claims to tribunal without the need to be dismissed first.

Possible exam and assignment questions. There are many possible ways in which exam and assignment questions can seek to explore discipline and grievance within HRM. The two main ways in which this topic might be found in a question are introduced here: first as a support theme for the main discussion purpose of the question and, secondly, as a theme in its own right. An example of the first type of question might be:

"Discuss the extent to which an appropriate organisational culture and management style would eliminate the need for a grievance procedure."

The answer to this question would require a discussion of culture, leadership and grievance procedures. The relationship between the three is a complex one and there is no easy answer possible. It could be argued that a 'good' (whatever that means) culture – presumably one in which managers cared for and were considerate of employees and their needs – would produce fewer dissatisfactions, complaints and grievances. On the other hand it could be argued that irrespective of such possibilities, because of human nature and the number of people (and hence interactions, personality clashes, personal likes and dislikes, personal aspirations, and so on) working in an organisation true harmony is an impossibility. In essence there is no right or wrong answer to this type of question as there are many different viewpoints. For a good answer it would be necessary to bring the various perspectives together and offer some conclusions based on the weight of argument and views of the individual answering the question.

An example of the second type of question might be:

"Critically evaluate the view that discipline and grievance procedures are an attempt to bring organisational justice to the employment relationship."

The answer to this question would begin with the material summarised in this section of the Companion. Organisational justice is about fairness and equity in seeking to ensure that both parties to the employment contract are happy with it in practice. Discipline is the means by which the employer seeks to ensure that the employee meets their responsibilities under the contract and the grievance procedure allows the employee to ensure that the employer meets their obligations. On the other hand power and control are never far from any discussion about management and the direction and channelling of employee behaviour. Discipline can be regarded as the tool to ensure employee compliance with management wishes and the grievance procedure the mechanism preventing management from going too far in this respect. For a good mark it would be necessary to explore all sides of the argument and then to propose a reasoned conclusion based on the weight of argument and the views of the individual answering the question.

Textbook Guide

ARMSTRONG: *Chapter 58.*

BEARDWELL, CLAYDON AND BEARDWELL: *Various chapters make reference to this topic.*

BLOISI: *Various chapters make some reference to this topic.*

FOOT AND HOOK: *Chapters 14 and 15.*

LEOPOLD, HARRIS AND WATSON: *Chapter 9.*

MARCHINGTON AND WILKINSON: *Various chapters make some reference to this topic.*

PILBEAM AND CORBRIDGE: *Chapters 17, 18 and 19.*

REDMAN AND WILKINSON: *Chapter 14.*

TORRINGTON, HALL AND TAYLOR: *Chapters 9, 15 and 25.*

2.10	
equality and diversity	

The legal framework

The law seeks to ensure that employers do not discriminate against particular categories of employee. It seeks to ensure that management decisions and actions are applied fairly and consistently across all current and potential employees. The major areas of legislation cover all aspects of the employment relationship including resourcing, reward, career development, pension and termination rights. The main areas covered by the requirement for equality of treatment are:

- Gender, marital status or sexual orientation.
- Disability.
- Race, national origin or ethnicity.
- Religion or belief.
- Ex-offenders with spent convictions.
- Membership (or non-membership) of a trade union.
- Part-time or **fixed-term contract** workers.

In general terms there are categories of discrimination that have been recognised by the legislation:

1 **Direct discrimination**. This occurs when the employer directly uses, say, sex or race as a decision variable. For example, an employer who advertised for a male computer operator would be directly discriminating against females – unless they could show that there existed a 'genuine occupational qualification', such as the need to have a female actor play a female part in a film.

2 **Indirect discrimination**. This occurs when a 'requirement or condition' for a job is set in such a way as to disadvantage a particular category of people. For example, advertising a job as being open to people over six feet tall would indirectly discriminate against women since a for greater proportion of men are over that height than are women.

3 **Positive discrimination**. This represents the situation where an employer seeks to overcome previous discrimination by giving preference to the group previously discriminated against. An example, would be seeking only women applicants for senior jobs in order to increase the proportion of females at that level. Such actions would be unlawful under UK law, although it would be permissible to adopt 'positive action' to prepare and encourage more women to apply for such jobs.

4 **Victimisation**. This refers to situations in which the employer seeks revenge or to take action against an employee (or group) because they sought to (or assist others to) claim their legal rights. For example, an employer might be found to have victimised an employee (by failing to promote them) because they had recently raised an equal pay claim.

Think about it?

Can legislation ever provide other than compliance approach to equality? Does that matter? Justify your answer.

Equal opportunities or diversity?

Equality of opportunity as discussed so far and as viewed in terms of legislation is about management decision making in relation to specific categories of people. In a practical sense it is about inappropriate decision making. In most situations it does not matter if an employee is male, black, Asian, female, married and so on, and the legislation seeks to encourage and prevent such irrelevant factors from being taken into account when they have no real bearing on the job or how it is done. Also, such factors should not have an impact on the level of reward, promotion, access to development opportunities or any other aspect of employment and so must be disregarded.

However, unfortunately all management decision making in relation to employees involves the requirement to discriminate between people in some way or another. For example, if ten people apply for one vacancy then nine people will be discriminated against as they will not be selected for the post. Equal opportunities seek to ensure that such decisions are not made using inappropriate factors, while recognising that some basis for selection is unavoidable.

Diversity is often taken to mean the same as equal opportunities. The argument underlying this view broadly is that by providing equality of opportunity for most categories of people in society then a diverse workforce matching the composition of society will be achieved along with fairness. However, as should be obvious from the discussion so far, equal opportunities is grounded in legislative provision and that is not the same as recognising the diversity of possible categorisations of people that exist in society. 'Equal opportunities' (as embraced in law) is based on categories defined by legislators and does not cover every possible manifestation of unfair discrimination. It is the broader interpretation implied by diversity that can inform a different approach to the debate. For example, people differ in terms of personality characteristics, political belief, team role preferences and so on – all of which might be expected to have some impact on organisational effectiveness.

Consequently the management of diversity is about the recognition that everyone differs from every other person in some way or another and that high performance organisational activity can be effectively achieved through the harnessing of that potential. As such, it represents a results-based approach to difference in people whereas it could be argued that the equal opportunities approach represents a moral approach to fairness in employment.

Think about it?

Is the business results approach to diversity or the legislative approach to equality more appropriate to an organisational context? Why?

Approaches to equality

The starting point for the equal opportunities approach is to identify groups that are disadvantaged in some way or another. In practice that can start with the realisation that a particular group from society dominates (or is largely absent from) some aspect of the job market; for example, the realisation that commercial airline pilots are predominantly male. This, it is argued, is wrong and unfair and that (all things being equal) everyone in a particular society should have an equal chance of gaining access to education, jobs, reward and career opportunities to the extent that their innate abilities and training would qualify them. Legislation is the primary means of underpinning the equality rights of disadvantaged minority groups and of ensuring the compliance of employers. In this form it is about equality of opportunity rather than equality of achievement. In other words it seeks to ensure that the particular 'category' of the individual is ignored when employment-related decisions are taken, under threat of penalty. It does not suggest that such individuals have preference in the allocation of jobs and so on. It is about encouraging people and using positive action to support previously disadvantaged people in overcoming discrimination.

It is argued by some that change must be forced onto organisations so that they actively recruit and promote people from previously disadvantaged groups. In doing so quotas and positive discrimination need to be used to forcibly change previous discriminatory practice, thus ensuring that disadvantaged groups quickly spread throughout the workforce. As an approach this is argued by its supporters to speed up the rate of change and the position of minority groups. However, by the opponents of such perspectives, it is said to restrict the ability of organisations to select and promote the best individuals through the requirement to **socially engineer** the workforce profile.

The main emphasis of the equal opportunities approach is that of seeking to further the interests of disadvantaged groups. It is not an approach which is concerned with individuals, but with company policy and practice on providing the opportunity for disadvantaged groups to overcome whatever has hindered access to areas of work that have previously been denied to them.

Think about it?

The law requiring equal pay was introduced some 30 years ago but a significant gap in earnings between men and women still exists. Why might this be so and what does it suggest about legislative approaches to equality? To what extent could equality be achieved without legislation?

Managing diversity

Diversity management is the recognition that individuals invariably differ in many ways and that the future success of an organisation can be improved if that 'difference' can be harnessed appropriately. There are organisations which place great store on achieving a high degree of uniformity among staff in terms of profile, attitudes and other characteristics. The main advantage to emerge from uniformity is that people will tend to think and act in similar ways, providing a greater level of organisational consistency than might otherwise be the case. This should make it easier to manage and provide consistency in service to customers. However, it can also have disadvantages in that it can encourage a 'clone' mentality, which if taken too far can result in the organisation losing an understanding of – and hence a connection to – the diversity in its markets. The survival of the organisation could be put at risk in this situation as it can be very difficult and take a long time to change the status quo.

Think about it?

Janis (1982) coined the term 'groupthink' in the 1960s. What is it and how does it relate to diversity as used in the current discussion?

Recognition of the commercial dangers that high levels of conformity can bring has led to the view that there is advantage and strength from achieving diversity. The problem comes in defining what 'difference' means in this context and how much of it should be allowed. Some of the organisational applications of the term diversity include:

- A commercially driven means of meeting equality legislation requirements.
- A means of matching the customer profile in an attempt to more effectively align business capability with customer needs and expectations.
- Recognition that conformity holds dangers and that diversity can provide a degree of robustness in business functioning.
- Recognition that if diversity can be better understood and more effectively managed it can contribute to the achievement of high performance working and a greater commercial success.

The foregoing reasons for adopting diversity do not answer questions about what difference means in an individual context, nor how much of each element of difference is appropriate to a specific job or context. To consider the first question, people 'differ' in many ways – height, weight, gender, ethnic grouping, intelligence, skill range, to identify just a few. Some of the ways in which people differ might have work-related or commercial benefit to an organisation and many will not have. For example, it would be difficult to make a case for the height of an employee having any relevance to the job that they do. Religious belief on the other hand may not have relevance to the job someone does in the UK, but there are some locations where this does not hold and so thought might need to be given to this aspect of 'difference'. It is very difficult to answer the question about what differences are relevant to an organisational activity, and much thought and research needs to be given to it if it is to be taken beyond the legal requirement level of consideration. It is about seeking to identify the 'things' that provide a potential contribution and benefit to the organisation.

The issue of 'how much' difference is appropriate is a very difficult question to answer. For some aspects of difference it is an irrelevant question; for example, how many left-handed people to employ – as many as present themselves as the best candidates is the answer. But in other cases of difference the answer is less obvious. Belbin (1993) argues that a balanced team composition is necessary if teams are to have a positive impact on company performance. Perhaps organisations should recruit, train and promote people with specific team roles in order to ensure that teams function effectively in creating success.

Think about it?

How practical might it be to apply team profile requirements as part of diversity management practice? What does this imply about diversity management in practice?

Diversity and culture

The basis of discrimination lies with the primeval recognition of differences and is significant in the perpetuation of domination of one group over others. Consequently, if diversity and equality of opportunity are to be achieved then the cultural issues and perspectives have to be addressed. Culture is important to diversity in two main ways:

1. Culture has an impact on how people react to and deal with people who are 'different' in some way or another.

2. The culture of minority groups is also an important determinant of their norms of behaviour, attitudes and expectations. For example, it is argued that men and women are different in their use of language, thinking and approaches to problem solving. Consequently, a process of adaptation or accommodation between cultures and ways of human functioning are required in order to integrate different people into a cohesive organisational unit.

This view of culture in relation to diversity suggests a move towards the group level of analysis rather than a clear focus on the individual and their needs/ability to contribute. It may encourage the view that the individual should adapt to the existing culture, not that the existing culture should adapt to meet the opportunities presented by a 'different' person. The natural tendency is for the dominant group to seek adaptation to their preferred culture and mode of functioning – but that leads to uniformity, which has its own dangers. It was suggested earlier that strength can come from capturing diversity effectively which can lead to a greater resilience in terms of the ability to respond to challenging social, trading and economic conditions.

Organisational approaches to equality and diversity

There are three basic approaches that can be taken to the issues of equality and diversity – based on LaFasto (1992):

1 *Compliance*. React to pressure and legal requirement. No real belief in the concepts or understanding the possible contribution from 'different' people.

2 *Managing*. Regards diversity as a useful business approach. Can see advantages in seeking to stay ahead of legislation and of going beyond the basics in search of commercial advantage.

3 *Valuing*. A genuine belief that employees represent the most important asset and resource for the business. A belief that the level of self-esteem of each individual is an important element in their level of commitment to the aims and objectives of the organisation, and so to their performance. A recognition that valuing people is the only way to achieve a high performance organisation.

Jackson et al. (1992) suggest a slightly different way in which organisations respond to diversity, emphasising the cultural aspect of the **organisational development** stages:

1 Level 1

- Stage 1: the exclusionary organisation. Seeks to maintain the status quo and the dominant groups seek to exclude others.
- Stage 2: the club. Seeks to maintain the position of the dominant group but is prepared to moderate that by allowing 'outsiders' to join providing they conform to the existing norms.

2 *Level 2*

- Stage 3: the compliance organisation. Seeks to adopt a minimalist approach by complying with legislative requirements. May encourage equality of opportunity at the lower levels but the dominant groups at the top remain largely unaffected.
- Stage 4: the affirmative action organisation. Actively seeks to change attitudes and adapt to changing circumstances through the development of people from minority groups.

3 *Level 3*

- Stage 5: the redefining organisation. Seeks to ensure that the culture of the organisation supports a multicultural workforce and that power is redistributed across all groups.
- Stage 6: the multicultural organisation. This level of achievement in cultural change recognises that everyone contributes and is a full member of the organisation. There is also recognition of the existence of a broader social responsibility, to encourage the development of other organisations and individuals and to seek to work on external sources of oppression.

Ross and Schneider (1992) suggest that organisational approaches to diversity are based on the following criteria:

- They originate from internal intentions rather than external requirement.
- They are focussed on individual rather than group levels of activity.
- They are focussed on the cultural aspects of organisational activity rather than on procedures, processes and systems.
- They are the responsibility of every function and person in the organisation, not just an HR policy.

They suggest a six-step process for achieving a diversity culture within the organisation:

1 *Diagnosis.* Identify what exists in relation to culture and levels of diversity – it identifies the baseline from which to move forward.

2 *Set the aims.* Justify a business case (also set the aims, objectives and outcomes) for the proposed change as well identifying senior level sponsors.

3 *Spread ownership.* Raise awareness of the benefits of diversity among everyone within the organisation. Encourage individuals at

all levels to question their attitudes and preconceptions about diversity. Move ownership towards everyone rather than just within the HR function.

4 *Policy development.* Involve everyone in policy development after some degree of widespread ownership is achieved. New procedures need the support of everyone to be effective.

5 *Managing the transition process.* Include activities such as training, **positive action** programmes, policy implementation and cultural awareness/change.

6 *Maintain momentum.* Measure and celebrate achievements; introduce initiatives to keep progress flowing.

Think about it?

Think about culture change as a process and also in relation to achieving a diversity culture. What specific actions might you seek to adopt during steps 3, 5 and 6 outlined above? How long might the entire six-step process take?

Possible exam and assignment questions. There are many possible ways in which exam and assignment questions can seek to explore equality and diversity within HRM. The two main ways in which this topic might be found in a question are introduced here: first as a support theme for the main discussion purpose of the question and, secondly, as a theme in its own right. An example of the first type of question might be:

"Resourcing decisions are based on the need to find the best candidate for the job based on job descriptions and person specifications. It is therefore impossible to achieve diversity in practice because the type of person being sought is predetermined. Critically evaluate this statement."

The answer to this question would require a discussion of culture, diversity and the resourcing process. The relationship between them is a complex one and there is no easy answer. The debate surrounds the organisational requirement to have certain tasks done by the new employee and the resourcing process which seeks to identify eligible people without discrimination creeping into the process. However, the diversity approach suggests that beyond a basic requirement there *could well be significant advantage to be gained by seeking how the job and organ-isational constraints could be flexed in order to accommodate a 'different' person. There would appear to be an inherent contradiction, therefore, in the established resourcing and the opportunity to adopt diversity as the guiding principle in an organisation. In essence there is no right or wrong answer to this type of question as there so many different viewpoints. For a good answer, it would be necessary to bring the various aspects of the discussion together and offer some conclu-sions based on the weight of argument and views of the individual answering the question.*

An example of the second type of question might be:

❝Outline the process for achieving a diversity culture within the organisation, developed by Ross and Schneider (1992).❞

The answer to this question would begin with the relevant material summarised in this section of the Companion. It would then need to be elaborated in order to demonstrate that the answer was not a simple repetition of the six steps which had been previously committed to memory. Remember that for a good mark you need to be able to show understanding, not just an ability to regurgitate material committed to memory. In this type of question, understanding could be demon-strated by including an elaboration or interpretation of the basic steps; incorpo-rating material surrounding the basic steps including examples of how these might have been used in practice and so on. It could also be demonstrated through the inclusion of contradictory arguments that might be used to show that the weaknesses in the diversity approach could be overcome through adopting an equal opportunity based approach.

Textbook Guide

ARMSTRONG: *Various chapters make some reference to this topic.*
BEARDWELL, CLAYDON AND BEARDWELL: *Chapter 7.*
BLOISI: *Chapter 11.*
FOOT AND HOOK: *Various chapters make some reference to this topic.*
LEOPOLD, HARRIS AND WATSON: *Chapter 5.*
MARCHINGTON AND WILKINSON: *Chapter 13.*
PILBEAM AND CORBRIDGE: *Chapter 8.*
REDMAN AND WILKINSON: *Chapters 12 and 13.*
TORRINGTON, HALL AND TAYLOR: *Chapters 23 and 24.*

2.11	
health, safety and welfare	

The scope of health, safety and welfare at work

Although the level of accidents and injuries at work has fallen dramatically over the past few decades it is still a significant factor in the lives of many people as the following sample of health and safety statistics from the Health and Safety Executive (HSE) website (accessed January 2007) shows:

Key HSE figures for 2005–2006

Ill health:

- *2 million people suffering from an illness they believed was caused or made worse by work.*
- *523,000 of these were new cases in the last 12 months.*
- *1,969 died of mesothelioma (2004), and thousands more from other occupational cancers and lung diseases.*

Injuries:

- *212 workers were killed at work, a rate of 0.7 per 100,000 workers.*
- *146,076 injuries were reported under RIDDOR, a rate of 562.4 per 100,000 employees.*
- *328,000 reportable injuries occurred, a rate of 1,200 per 100,000 workers (2004–2005).*

Working days lost

- *30 million days were lost overall (1.3 days per worker), 24 million due to work-related ill health and 6 million due to workplace injury.*

Although the above figures are significant, the same site shows that the level of accidents and injury reduced significantly between 1974 and 2006:

- The number of fatal injuries fell by 76 per cent.
- The rate of fatal injury (per 100,000 employees) fell by 79 per cent.

- The number of non-fatal injuries fell by 68 per cent.
- There have been reductions in injury rates across all sectors.
- Around 24 per cent of the reduction in the rate of fatal injury in the last ten years can be attributed to a shift in employment away from manufacturing and heavy industry to lower risk service industries.
- About 50 per cent of the reduction in non-fatal injury rate since 1986 is due to changes in the occupations of workers.

The scope of heath, safety and welfare at work is anything that can harm (actually or potentially) anyone who comes into contact in any way with the organisation, its products or services. Its purpose is to identify and manage the risk and possible consequences for all parties.

Think about it?

How could you differentiate between having fun at work and engaging in potentially harmful horseplay? What might management do to encourage fun but prevent accidents?

The business case for health and safety at work

The business case for taking health and safety at work seriously is based around four factors:

1 Illness and injury originating from work-related causes lead to absence which could otherwise be avoided. Such absence increases cost (including sick pay and providing replacement labour) and reduces productivity.

2 Illness and injury due to work-related factors lead to claims for financial compensation.

3 A poor health and safety reputation leads to high labour turnover as existing staff leave as soon as they get the opportunity and difficulty is experienced in recruiting good quality replacements.

4 The reputation for poor health and safety leads to the employer being regarded as a weak, probably inconsistent supplier who cannot be trusted to deliver high quality goods or services. Negative publicity can arise for organisations not paying attention to the health and safety record of its suppliers.

While the business case for taking health and safety at work seriously is compelling, there is also a legislative requirement to do so.

Think about it?

If the business case is clear, why are there still so many accidents, injuries and health problems indicated in the data provided above from the HSE?

The Health and Safety Commission and Health and Safety Executive

The body charged with oversight of legislative provision and the policing of its requirements is the Health and Safety Commission whose functions include those listed below.

- To make arrangements to secure the health, safety and welfare of people at work and the public in the way that undertakings are conducted, including: proposing new laws and standards, conducting, research, providing information and advice, and controlling explosives and other dangerous substances. This also includes promulgating Codes of Practice through the HSE.
- To maintain the Employment Medical Advisory Service (EMAS) which provides advice on occupational health matters.

The Health and Safety Commission also appoints the Health and Safety Executive (HSE) which has two main functions:

1 To advise and assist the Health and Safety Commission carry out its obligations.

2 To enforce health and safety law.

HSE inspectors have considerable power to visit premises without notice to inspect work activity and equipment. They are able to:

1 *Issue warnings or give advice*, making suggestions for improvement where no immediate risk to life or heath is apparent.

2 *Issue improvement or prohibition notices.* Improvement notices allow current arrangements to continue as long as specified changes to equipment or work practices are made within a specified timescale. Prohibition notices require current work to stop immediately – as it is considered too great a risk to health or safety to continue – and not to

recommence until remedial action has been taken. In both cases appeal against the notice issued is possible.

3 *Prosecute* those held responsible in the criminal courts for serious offences, including initiating a police investigation for manslaughter in the case of a death at work.

4 *Conduct investigations* of accidents or incidents at work in order to learn lessons or prepare legal action.

Legislative provision and civil remedies in health and safety

Legislative provision

Legislation has two main approaches in that some provisions are:

1 *Mandatory.* For example, a mine must always have two exits. There is a duty on all employers to assess risk and take appropriate action.

2 *Advisory.* Responsibilities are expressed as goals or targets and are to be achieved 'so far as is reasonably practical' or through exercising 'adequate *control*'. The requirement here is that any risk should be identified and eliminated or minimised unless the cost or difficulty is disproportionate to the degree of risk identified.

The enforcement of legislation falls to either a local authority or the HSE through its inspectors.

The current major legislation in the UK covering health and safety at work is the Health and Safety at Work Act (1974). This brought together and updated previous legislation and has as its main purposes:

- To secure the health, safety and welfare of people at work.
- To protect the public from risks associated with workplace activity.
- To control the use and storage of dangerous substances.
- To control potentially dangerous emissions into the environment.
- To ensure that managers and employees take their responsibilities for health, safety and welfare seriously. Managers have a clear responsibility for the development and implementation of appropriate policy. Employees have a legal obligation to ensure their own health, safety and welfare and that of others by following safety rules and using safety equipment provided. Recognised trade unions also have the right to appoint safety representatives with whom managers must consult about health and safety matters.

The following is the legislative and regulatory provision that is the responsibility of, and enforced by, the HSE:

- A wide range of legislation predating 1974, such as the Celluloid and Cinematograph Film Act (1922); Employment of Women, Young Persons, and Children Act (1920); and the Explosives Act (1875).
- Health and Safety at Work Act (1974).
- The First Aid Regulations (1981), which requires the provision of appropriate first aid equipment and facilities.
- The Control of Substances Hazardous to Health (COSHH) Regulations (1988) as amended in 2002, 2003 and 2004. This set of regulations covers the storage, use and control of any substance that is a known hazard to health.
- The Management of Health and Safety at Work Regulations (1992). This incorporated of a number of European Directives into UK law, including the use of protective equipment, manual handling, display screen equipment and protection for pregnant women.
- The Health and Safety (Consultation with Employees) Regulations (1996). Makes provision for employee consultation over health and safety matters where there is no trade union recognised.
- Working Time Regulations (1998). Incorporated aspects of European legislation on working time into UK law.
- In addition, some 190 other regulations (as at January 2007) that cover specific industries or aspects of work that are 'owned and enforced' by the HSE.

The HSE also produces about 70 publications including books, statutory instruments, approved codes of practice and guides to legislative requirement.　　　．

Civil remedies

These remedies rely on the common law and the law of contract. Someone who is injured or whose health is adversely affected by what they claim were their work experiences can sue their employer for an implied breach of the duty of care or of the employer's duty to provide safe systems of work. It is also possible for the employee to use the law of tort if they can show that an employer had been negligent or had breached a statutory duty. In order to succeed in any claim it would be necessary for an employee to show that the employer had acted unreasonably and that the injury (or damage) had occurred in the course of their employment.

Vicarious liability can also arise in that the negligent actions of one employee, which then adversely impact on another, are the responsibility of the employer. Also impacting on courts' decisions as to liability will be the actions of the injured party who may have contributed, to some degree, to their own condition. For example, a claim that a chest complaint was the result of noxious fumes at work may not be accepted as the sole cause if injury if the employee was also a heavy smoker.

> **Think about it?**
>
> *Given the range of regulation on health and safety matters, to what extent is it possible for any manager to know their obligations with regard to such issues?*

Safety committees and safety representatives

Safety committees can help management to develop, promote, monitor and update their health and safety management systems. They should:

- Develop safe systems of work and safety procedures.
- Analyse accidents and causes of notifiable occupational diseases.
- Review risk assessments.
- Examine safety audit reports.
- Consider reports submitted by safety representatives.
- Monitor the effectiveness of health and safety training.
- Consider reports and factual information provided by HSE inspectors and environmental health officers.
- Monitor and review the adequacy of health and safety communication and publicity within the workplace.
- Continuously monitor all arrangements for health and safety and revise them whenever necessary.

Managers and employee representatives should agree who chairs the meetings, how often meetings should be held, how the committee should undertake its responsibilities and what they intend to achieve.

The Safety Representatives and Safety Committees Regulations (1977) set out the responsibilities and legal functions of safety representatives, which include:

- Representing employees in discussions with the employer on health, safety or welfare issues and in discussions with the HSE or other enforcing authorities.
- Being consulted 'in good time' over a large range of health and safety issues.
- Being involved with risk assessment procedures.
- Attending safety committee meetings.
- Having access to relevant health and safety information.
- Inspecting the workplace.

- Investigating potential hazards.
- Investigating notifiable accidents, cases of disease or ill health, and dangerous occurrences.
- Investigating employees' complaints.
- Receiving information from health and safety inspectors.
- Being given paid time off their normal work to carry out their functions and undergo training.
- Having access to suitable facilities and assistance to carry out their functions.

Employee welfare

1 *Emotional welfare*. These are difficult issues to identify and deal with largely because they are internal to the individual and the symptoms may not be easily detected until a crisis arises. They include:

- Management style. An aggressive approach to the management of employees can lead to stress and emotional breakdown if it is a permanent feature of work.
- **Bullying**. Examples include an aggressive management style, and the inappropriate behaviour of colleagues, customers, suppliers and subordinates.
- **Harassment**. Broadly, this is seeking to pressure another person into doing something that they would prefer not to do. The effect on the target is to cause (among other things) emotional stress.
- Performance management. Badly designed systems, unrealistically high targets, aggressive management styles and blame-oriented performance reviews cause emotional stress.
- Working conditions. Poor job design; short-cycle, repetitive work routines; emotionally and physically demanding work; dangerous work. For example, foundry work involves exposure to furnace level temperatures and the risk from molten metal spillages.
- Work routines and processes. Hard physical work can be emotionally draining; some jobs are boring and offer little opportunity for variation in the work routine. For example, dealing with customer complaints is demanding with high levels of **stress**.
- Stress. Can result from any of the issues discussed above and relates to emotional and physical responses to the conditions experienced. It may also be caused by events outside of work but have an effect on the individual's work.

All of these forms of emotional welfare have an impact on health and safety at work. The employer is required by legislation to identify the level of risk and to take appropriate action to elimi-nate or minimise it. There is also a business case for seeking to minimise the dangers from these issues as it will contribute to the well-being of employees and consequently the performance of the business.

2 *Physical welfare.* Providing for the physical welfare of employees takes many forms including:

- Work design. Making the work safe to do through careful equip-ment design and also by the careful design of work routines, pro-cedures and practices. Working times – with rules on shift work, overtime and holiday entitlement – can also have an impact on the physical well-being of the employee.
- Job and related training. Training employees to understand cor-rect lifting and other effective work practices can significantly reduce accidents at work.
- Safety training. Training employees on health and safety issues can significantly impact on their approach to work.
- Benefit package provision. Many elements within the employee ben-efits package are relevant to the physical welfare of employees. For example, health screening can identify early signs of medical condi-tions that might impact on future work ability and offer the oppor-tunity for preventive treatment. Sick pay, incapacity pensions and holiday provision also have an impact on the way that well-being is managed.

Think about it?

Comprehensive welfare provision within an organisation maximises employee commitment and contribution. To what extent and how might this claim be substantiated?

Employee assistance programmes

Employee assistance programmes (EAP) can provide support across a wide range of difficulties and problems in people's lives which might impact on work performance. The basic model is that the employer provides an external source of support and advice for its employees to make use of at their discretion. Such providers are specialist consultancies which offer a variety of support services to organisations, for a fee. The employee would not be charged for a predetermined level of support and the employer would not be told of any specific contact made by an employee or what the nature of the contact was. The most common level of support is a telephone counselling/advice service available 24 hours a day. That can be supported by (if the employer or employee pays for it) meetings with psychologists or specialist counsellors to provide personal support.

Obviously the EAP provider would have to give some information (total number of contacts, types of issue) to the employer to justify the fee, but would not divulge enough information to identify any particular employee. Common issues referred to EAP providers include:

* Marital or relationship problems.
* Emotional problems.
* Family problems.
* Housing problems.
* Consumer problems.
* Depression/anxiety problems.
* Financial problems.
* Work-related problems.
* Stress/pressure problems.

Occupational health departments

Larger organisations may have an **occupational health department** that would be charged with oversight of health and safety at work. The range of services available could include any or all of the following:

* Emergency treatment beyond simple first aid.
* Medical, dental, optician treatments where outside appointments might conflict with work duties.
* Advice to management in relation to work-related medical matters.
* Monitoring of incidents by a safety officer to identify hazards and risk.
* Health screening for prospective employees and regular check-ups for all employees.
* Contribution to training programmes.
* Monitoring HSE and EMAS publications and requirements.

Risk assessment

According to the HSE website (accessed January 2007), sensible **risk management** is about:

- Ensuring that workers and the public are properly protected.
- Providing overall benefit to society by balancing benefits and risks, with a focus on reducing frequent or serious risks.
- Enabling innovation and learning.
- Ensuring that those who create risks manage them responsibly and understand that failure to manage them will lead to robust action
- Enabling individuals to understand that they have to exercise responsibility

Sensible risk management is not about:

- Creating a totally risk-free society.
- Generating useless paperwork mountains.
- Scaring people by exaggerating trivial risks.
- Stopping recreational and learning activities where the risks are managed.
- Reducing protection of people from risks that cause real harm and suffering.

The same website also suggests a five-step process to assess the risks in any workplace:

Step 1: **Identify** the hazards
Step 2: **Decide** who might be harmed and how
Step 3: **Evaluate** the risks and decide on precaution
Step 4: **Record** your findings and implement them
Step 5: **Review** your assessment and update if necessary

Think about it?

To what extent is the identification and management of risk the key skill that any manager should acquire? Why?

Possible exam and assignment questions. There are many possible ways in which exam and assignment questions can seek to explore health, safety and welfare within HRM. The two main ways in which this topic might be found in a question are introduced here: firstly as a support theme for the main discussion purpose of the question and, secondly, as a theme in its own right. An example of the first type of question might be:

"Discuss the extent to which poor reward system design might contribute to health, safety or welfare problems at work."

The answer to this question would require a discussion of reward system design, as well as aspects of health, safety and welfare. A discussion of the design of reward schemes and the ways that they might encourage bullying, and create pressure to achieve targets and salary reviews based on performance – and the effect on employee well-being – is what might be expected. The answer might system design might contribute to health, safety or welfare problems at work also involve a discussion of the duty of care as well as some of the other legislative requirements to assess risk of problems, as a result of the possible dangers of poor reward design. For a good answer it would be necessary to bring the various aspects of the discussion together and offer some conclusions based on the weight of argument and views of the individual answering the question.

An example of the second type of question might be:

"Outline the respective roles of the Health and Safety Commission and the Health and Safety Executive and explain the powers of inspectors."

The answer to this question would begin with the relevant material summarised in this section of the Companion. Remember that for a good mark you need to be able to show understanding, not just an ability to regurgitate material committed to memory. In this type of question, understanding could be demonstrated by including such features as an explanation or interpretation of the basic powers of inspectors and by discussing the emphasis on improvement rather than punishment. Also the balance between the requirement on both employer and employee to uphold the legislation and its intentions should be brought into the discussion. It is the quality of the discussion that would determine the mark awarded in such questions.

Textbook Guide

ARMSTRONG: *Chapters 55 and 56.*
BEARDWELL, CLAYDON AND BEARDWELL: *Chapter 12.*
BLOISI: *Chapter 10.*
FOOT AND HOOK: *Chapters 11 and 12.*

LEOPOLD, HARRIS AND WATSON: *Various chapters make some reference to this topic.*
MARCHINGTON AND WLKINSON: *Various chapters make some reference to this topic.*
PILBEAM AND CORBRIDGE: *Chapters 13 and 14.*
REDMAN AND WILKINSON: *Various chapters make some reference to this topic.*
TORRINGTON, HALL AND TAYLOR: *Chapter 22.*

2.12	
strategy and HRM	

Business strategy and HR strategy

One view of business strategy is that it is an approach to understanding what the future holds and thereafter deciding how the business should position itself relative to that 'known' future. The other possibilities for how strategy should be determined, if it can be determined at all, are:

1 Identify the future and use that information to guide business direction and activity; recognising that the future will change and that adaptation in company direction and activity will be needed to maintain alignment. Recognise that it might be possible to influence the future as well as the organisation's position relative to it.

2 This perspective holds that it is not possible to know the future with any certainty and so any view can only be a vague approximation. Consequently continuous short- medium-term scanning is necessary along with high levels of flexibility and adaptability in business activity. This represents the opportunistic view of strategy in relation to business activity.

Within these approaches to strategy, de Wit and Meyer (1999) suggest that there are three elements of strategy development:

1 *Strategy process.* The processes, procedures and techniques involved in developing strategy options.

2 *Strategy content.* The developed strategy for the organisation – the output from the process.

3 *Strategy context.* The organisational, industry and situational environments within which the strategy is to be implemented.

Whatever the organisation's view of strategy the HR function needs to be involved in the process as the HR policies need to align with business strategy. The range of possible relationships between business and HR strategy include (according to Torrington, Hall and Taylor, 2005):

1 *Separation.* This represents a separation between the business and people dimensions of organisational planning. The HR function (if one exists) is simply required to determine the short-term needs of the business and to deliver accordingly.

2 *Fit.* This represents a one-way process in which HR is given the output from the business strategy development process and has the opportunity to develop appropriate HR strategies to support it.

3 *Dialogue.* This recognises that there are advantages to allowing some communication between the HR and business strategy specialists during the business strategy development process.

4 *Holistic.* This recognises that there is a need to integrate business and HR strategy if success is to be achieved. It goes beyond dialogue and seeks the integration of the HR aspects into the business strategy development process.

5 *HR driven.* This represents a development on the previous approach in that HR strategy is allowed to shape the business strategy. It represents recognition that business success is dependant on people and that no business strategy can be effective without the active and willing contribution of employees at all levels.

Think about it?

To what extent should HR strategy be management driven or should it contain an employee perspective as well? If so how might that be achieved?

Is strategic HRM the same as HR strategy?

Strategy has been described by some writers as a form of organisational learning, creating an understanding of the various environments that the organisation is embedded within. That understanding then forms the basis of change within the organisation as it seeks to continually adjust and adapt to the evolving understanding of the future that emerges from the strategic process.

Whatever the degree of formality in the strategic process, if there is a connection between business strategy and HR strategy then it could be argued that **strategic HRM** is being practiced. However, without formalised association between the HR and business strategy, strategic HRM is absent. But that in itself does not mean that there is no HR strategy. For example, the HR management team in that context will have to work within those constraints and consequently develop HR policies that provide high levels of flexibility in the future. That in itself is an HR strategy in the sense of seeking to adopt a longer-term focus with the intention of positioning HR policy and practice to meet the needs of an undefined future.

Think about it?

How would you differentiate between a tactic and a strategy? Is the difference significant in the context of this discussion?

Perspectives on strategic HRM

There are four main models of strategic HRM that have emerged through the academic literature. They are:

1 *Best practice model.* Essentially based on Guest's prescriptive model of HRM (1989) which contains four HR policy objectives:

- Integration of HR into strategic planning process. Also implies that HRM policies are coherent and are used to inform line management practice.
- Commitment of employees to the organisation and high performance working.
- Flexibility in organisational structure and the use of employees through multi-skilling.
- Quality in the output of goods and services achieved through high calibre employees who are committed to the organisation and their work, and can offer high performance and flexibility.

2 *Harvard model.* Developed by Beer, Spector, Lawrence, Quinn Mills and Walton (1984) it has similarities with both the best practice and contingency models. It recognises that there are situational factors

which impact on the HR strategies choices that exist, but is prescriptive in that it envisages a predetermined set of HR outcomes that are universally valued.

3 *Contingency model.* Based on the idea that there is no single best model of strategic HR as the term 'best' can only be assessed in relation to the circumstances. It envisages two aspects that need to be incorporated into the assessment:

- The degree of 'fit' between the HR strategy and the business strategy.
- The degree of integration between HR policies and practices.

4 *Resource based model.* Any organisation comprises a collection of resources (including people) that need to be harnessed together in meeting the desired strategy. It emphasises the achievement of **competitive advantage** through the development of **human capital**, not just the alignment of HR with business strategy. To achieve competitive advantage through a particular resource it must be capable of meeting four criteria:

- Valuable. The resource must be capable of adding value to the organisation (to differentiate between competitors). Resourcing and development are important in identifying excellent people and ensuring that they are able to deliver value to the business.
- Scarcity. There is not an unlimited supply of any resource; it must be found and used with care and thought to extract maximum value in creating competitive advantage.
- Inimitable. It should not be possible to copy exactly the source and cause of competitive advantage in another firm. The unique combination of people, circumstances, relationships, history and how they are harnessed into the creation of competitive advantage should not be capable of replication by another organisation.
- Non-substitutable. No resource should be capable of being substituted by another. For example, it is relatively easy to replace people with technology. But technology is often incapable of the intelligent thought and action that a human can display when non-standard situations arise.

Human capital is an elusive term and it has been suggested that 'human capital' is on loan to the organisation as it is in large measure in the gift of employees to give or withhold, depending on the condition of the broader employment relationship.

Think about it?

Try to define human capital.

HR role in strategy formulation

The level of HR involvement in strategy formulation depends on the status of the function and the expectation that the board of directors has about the role of HR within company activity. For example, just because the head of HR is also a main board director it is no guarantee of close HR involvement in strategy development. Among the reasons that HR practitioners do not always play a significant role in strategy development are: they are not always regarded as having a business or strategic focus; lack understanding of business needs; or they are seen as not having the ability to understand and use business or financial terminology.

Each of the sections in this part of the book covers an aspect of HR management and as such each has a part to play in strategic development. For example, performance management is important to strategy but it is difficult to measure performance. It is relatively easy to create a measure (qualitative or quantitative) of performance for the job of a senior manager – profit and share price being obvious examples, though both are not totally under the control of senior managers. That approach to measurement of performance is frequently cascaded down throughout the organisation. However, being a 'top-down' approach it is not always the most appropriate means of measuring performance. For example, in a call centre the management might view performance in terms of number of calls dealt with, but phone operators might regard their job as dealing with customer problems – so making customers happy might be seen as the real purpose of the job from their perspective. Customer satisfaction or volume of repeat business might be more appropriate measures of performance from an employee (and customer) perspective. These and similar points all need to be debated as part of the development of strategic perspective associated with performance management. The same need for intelligent debate is true of each aspect of HR activity within the organisation if the contribution to strategy is to be effective.

Measuring the contribution of HR to the business

Identifying the specific contribution of HR to an organisation is difficult as there are so many other influences active in the situation at the same time. In most organisations HR carries no direct responsibility for the management of people or for the achievement of business objectives; therefore, their contribution is usually indirect, facilitative and supportive. For example, the introduction of an absence control policy might result in the reduction in absence of some 60 per cent over the first year, but how much of the responsibility for that can be claimed by the HR department? HR may have developed the policy in consultation with the trade unions, employees and line managers; they may also have trained line managers in how to conduct absence monitoring and associated interviews, discipline handling and so on. But it would be line managers who would actually implement the policy and carry out the necessary monitoring and follow-up work. It would also be the employees who responded positively to the new initiative by not taking as much 'sick leave' as previously. In such situations how could the actual impact of the HR function be apportioned other than as a qualitative statement along the lines that 'we developed an absence policy which has resulted (due to the actions of others) in the reduction of absence by 60 per cent'. Conversely, line managers would be able to claim that by their actions they had reduced absence by 60 per cent which had produced a reduction in overtime and other additional labour cost of x per cent and/or an increase in output of y per cent.

Kaplan and Norton (1992) developed their balanced business scorecard using four sets of factors – financial measures; customer measures; internal business process measures; and learning and growth measures – a model that has been applied to the HR function. Becker et al. (2001) suggested the necessity for a measurement system that allowed HR to demonstrate its effect on business performance. The need exists to avoid the function being viewed as marginal and a suitable candidate for **outsourcing**. They suggest a seven-step process to identify and measure HR's contribution:

1 Engage with business strategy development in a way that requires discussion of how it can be implemented and communicated across the organisation.

2 Develop a business case for HR to be regarded as a strategic asset that can facilitate business strategy development and implementation.

3 Create a strategy map for each area of the business, showing how each area needs an HR contribution to deliver appropriate employee behaviours, attitudes and performance.

4 Identify HR deliverables for the strategic plan and map, for example, **labour turnover** and absence rates, articulating the need for HR input to them.

5 Align HR policy development and sub-functions with the deliverables from the previous stage.

6 Design a strategic HR measurement system that allows for valid measures of the deliverables achieved.

7 Adopt management by measurement against the deliverables identified.

Think about it?

How could you measure the performance of an HR department?

The traditional form of the HR function was an in-house department headed by a senior manager or director with a number of professional HR and administrative staff to support the running of the department. The structure of the department would depend on a number of issues such as the size and structure of the company. However, these days a number of different approaches to the delivery of HR support to an organisation have evolved. They include decentralised, consultancy, outsourcing, e-HR and **service centre** detailed below:

1 *Decentralised support.* A small centralised HR department offering policy development, support and co-ordination, with HR units in each operating unit within the company reporting to the appropriate line manager. The intention is to maximise HR involvement with line departments by giving line managers greater control over HR activity, thereby preventing HR from becoming detached from the operational core of the business.

2 *Consultancy support.* Managing people is a line manager responsibility and the role of HR is to provide the means through which line managers are able to exercise that responsibility. Tends to be project based, aiming to analyse situations and to deliver to line managers enough procedural, policy and practical support to allow them to manage their employees more effectively. The basis for the delivery is the service-level agreement – a formal document specifying the nature of the support provided and against which performance can be measured.

3 *Outsourcing.* Involves sub-contracting the organisation's HR functions to a company specialising in the provision of HR services. The basis for the delivery of such services is the service-level agreement. Anything outside of the contract would be chargeable as an extra service attracting additional cost. The argument used in support of outsourcing is that specialist providers have high levels of expertise

in providing HR services at a lower cost than can be achieved in-house. However, the counter argument is that it is a less 'connected' service as the employees of the provider do not work for the host company and, unless the contract is drawn up very carefully, additional cost becomes inevitable.

Think about it?

What other aspects of outsourcing would need to be considered very carefully before any contract was agreed?

---

4 *e-HR.* Can take many forms including a service centre or the increased use of intranets and technology to deal with HR issues. It is not uncommon to find that, through such systems, employees can have direct access to their personnel files and a wide range of information about training and benefit package provision.

5 *Service centres.* Can be operated in-house or in partnership with other organisations. They operate like a help-desk (or service desk) for IT support. They are usually small in size (in comparison to a traditional in-house HR department) and offer direct advice and support either by phone or over the Internet. The structure and size of a service centre will depend on many factors including the size of the company and the geographic spread of business units.

Managing people – an HR or line management responsibility?

Every line manager has a responsibility for two major aspects of organisational activity. First there is the achievement of the business objectives set for the area. Secondly there is the management of the people that report to the line manager. Every manager with subordinates is a line manager. For example, the financial accountant would be the line manager for everyone working in the financial accounts department and the production manager would be the line manager for factory employees. Line management is different to a line department which are the operational departments and within the business. A line department is responsible for meeting the output requirements of the business. For example, in a manufacturing company the line departments would be those involved with the production of the goods offered for sale, or in a fast-food restaurant company it would be the retail outlets.

Line managers are responsible for achieving the objectives set for their departments, but these can only be achieved through their subordinates. That creates a difficulty in that each line manager must find ways of directing and channelling subordinate behaviour in pursuit of the manager's objectives. In that context the ability of the manager to achieve their objectives is based on a direct and dynamic working relationship with each employee. The organisation provides policies, procedures, work procedures, technology and so on, but objectives are achieved in the daily working dynamic between boss, subordinates and colleagues.

Because line managers are responsible for managing their own subordinates a major aspect of HR work is to convince line managers that they have something to contribute towards the effective management of people – a situation not always easy to achieve for many reasons. Most line managers have immediate objectives to achieve – a factory must meet its daily production schedule. But they also have longer-term objectives to achieve – ongoing cost reduction, for example. Equally, objectives might conflict with each other: for example, achieve higher levels of output with fewer quality faults and at lower cost. Such an objective might require employees to work harder and with greater flexibility, and less overtime and no pay rise. Not a situation that employees could be expected to support – conflict might be expected. It is working against this background that causes many line managers to yearn after quick, easy solutions and they can often resent what might appear to be longer-term, procedural, rule based and consultative 'jaw-jaw' approaches offered by HR. After all, telling a line manager with a problem today that adopting high performance working would help is not going to be well received – particularly if the HR specialist saying it is a relatively young social science graduate who has never 'got their hands dirty'! It is necessary for HR specialists to think about how they can maximise their credibility with line managers before they can expect to be taken seriously as business partners. Some of the possibilities for so doing include:

- Get to know the business and the people who work within it.
- Don't just quote procedure and legislative requirement to justify advice.
- Work alongside line managers and not remotely in an office, over the telephone or through a computer.
- Get to understand the pressures facing line managers.
- Recognise that line managers want practical solutions, not theory-based ones. But recognise the part that theory can play in identifying solutions.

- Recognise that the role of HR is usually to offer advice and guidance but it is a line manager responsibility to take action – an important distinction if damage limitation or crisis management becomes necessary as a consequence. Subsequent HR responses can enhance (or weaken) their credibility with line managers (and employees).

Think about it?

How else might you seek to maximise personal and professional credibility with line managers and employees?

Possible exam and assignment questions. There are many possible ways in which exam and assignment questions can seek to explore strategy within HRM. The two main ways in which this topic might be found in a question are introduced here: first as a support theme for the main discussion purpose of the question and, secondly, as a theme in its own right. An example of the first type of question might be:

"Resourcing is about finding the best people available to carry out particular jobs now, yet strategy demands a long-term perspective meaning that these two aspects of HR are incompatible. Discuss this statement."

The answer to this question would require a discussion of resourcing as well as the strategy related topics from this section. All resourcing is done against a specification of the qualities and competencies required of the individual and it goes without saying that these focus on current work activities. That can make it difficult to fill vacancies aimed at the long-term targets. However, identifying particular personality characteristics – people amenable to change and with a desire to do so – might enable them to adapt well to an uncertain future. For a good answer it would be necessary to bring the various aspects of the discussion together and offer some conclusions based on the weight of argument and views of the individual answering the question.

An example of the second type of question might be:

"Business functions in an increasing changeable and unstable world. Consequently the only viable HR strategy should be to maximise flexibility in all people management aspects of organisational functioning. Discuss this statement."

The answer to this question would begin with the relevant material summarised in this section of the Companion. Remember that for a good mark you need to be able to show understanding, not just an ability to regurgitate material committed to memory. In this type of question, understanding could be demonstrated by including such features as a discussion of what business strategy is and how it relates to HR strategy, both in general terms and in relation to specific HR areas of work. Also a discussion of the requirement on the employer to uphold company policy and employment legislation and its intentions should be brought into the discussion. It is the quality of the discussion that would determine the mark awarded in such questions.

Textbook Guide

ARMSTRONG: *Chapters 4, 5, 7, 8 and 9.*
BEARDWELL, CLAYDON AND BEARDWELL: *Chapter 12.*
BLOISI: *Chapter 12.*
FOOT AND HOOK: *Chapter 2.*
LEOPOLD, HARRIS AND WATSON: *Chapters 1, 4 and 16.*
MARCHINGTON AND WILKINSON: *Chapter 5.*
PILBEAM AND CORBRIDGE: *Chapters 2 and 5.*
REDMAN AND WILKINSON: *Chapter 8.*
TORRINGTON, HALL AND TAYLOR: *Chapters 2, 4, 10, 16, 20, 26 and 33.*

2.13

international HRM

Global strategy, local action

International organisational activity has existed in one form or another for many hundreds if not thousands of years. Each generation across history has brought with it different challenges and requirements in managing international organisations and in each case there would be associated people issues to take into account. The current approach to international business is to have a global strategy but with the capability to act locally. Human beings grow and develop in a particular cultural context and while there will be many similarities between every culture there are also many differences. The most basic definition of culture is, 'the way we do things around here'. It can be very difficult for any international organisation to arrange its affairs consistently across diverse operating locations. To be commercially successful, organisations that operate across borders need to be able to create effective and efficient methods of work; achieve operational, procedural and systems consistency; and also to have uniformity in management approach. The more diverse the organisation in location and international activity terms, the more difficult it becomes to achieve these requirements. So, while there are many advantages to being able to operate internationally, there are also difficulties and problems associated with doing so.

It is in seeking to achieve the conflicting requirements indicated above that the idea of global strategy and local action comes to the fore. Seeking to impose methods of working and perspectives from an outside and often remote headquarters is not always successful. Consequently, the idea of acting locally is an attempt to capitalise on local ways of doing things and so get the full benefit of geographic diversity. Global strategy represents the requirement to capture the individuality of operating conventions within a cohesive planning framework. HRM clearly has a major part to play in guiding and channelling the ways in which difference is harnessed so that overall unity of purpose, direction and commercial viability is achieved and maintained.

Think about it?

What are the differences between a multinational company and a global company, and what implications might this have for HRM activity?

International operations

There are many different forms that international activity can take, all of which have different implications for the HRM activities and approaches required. They include:

1. *The export of goods and services.* This form of international activity has very little HRM implication as in most instances the organisation itself is based in one location. Consequently, the HR policies

and practices adopted will be based on the home country norms with no need to cater for other country variations to be incorporated. The exception would be the need to provide HR policies covering employees who needed to deal with exports or visit other countries.

2 *Sales agents*. Requires less specialist HRM support than direct exporting as the agent would usually be paid commission for sales achieved but would not be a direct employee.

3 *Licensing or franchising*. Involves an agreement between the company and a license or franchise holder to run a 'mini-business' in a particular location in return for a fee or proportion of the profit. The originating company will make provision to support the license or franchise holder with business management support (including HRM) as part of the agreement. There would be a need to ensure the provision of appropriate HRM advice and support to its local licensees or franchisees.

4 *Management contracts*. This involves running something on behalf of someone else in return for a fee. Someone in Singapore might own a hotel building and employ an established hotel group to run it on their behalf. It would be necessary for the contractor to have an ability to recruit, train and generally manage employees in each location that they hold a management contract.

5 *Technical assistance agreements*. In practice these are similar to the management contracts, but they tend to be used for consultancy or knowledge transfer situations. In HR terms there would be a need to cater for expatriate labour as well as helping to develop appropriate local HR arrangements.

6 *Contract manufacturing*. This type of arrangement involves the subcontracting of part of the organisation's process to a local business. For example, a car manufacturer might subcontract engine making to a company based in another country with cheaper labour. In HR terms this type of arrangement has little direct impact other than the requirement to train company staff in how to negotiate deals across cultures, understand the demands of customs and freight systems, and monitor local labour practice.

7 *Partnership/joint venture direct investment*. Involves working with local partners or through joint ventures with other companies entering another country. Any local partner should have expertise in local HRM polices and practices. There is a need to be able to ensure an appropriate balance between local and home company HR practices as it is possible that the local partner might seek to 'shift the balance' in favour of local circumstances.

8 *Directly owned investment.* This type of investment involves the company investing directly in another country. It involves the HR specialists in developing an understanding of the local conditions and in being able to create an HRM framework that matches the needs of local and home company conditions.

In addition to the types of international business, different forms of **organisational structure** can be created to support business activity including:

1 *Geographic divisional structure.* Involves each country (or region) being a separate business entity in its own right within the overall corporate structure. Each division might have a full set of business functions (including HR) under the leadership of a divisional manager.

2 *International divisional structure.* All international activities of the business would be amalgamated within a single international division.

3 *Product structure.* Each type of product or service would form the basis of a division. For example, an automotive division; an aircraft division; a general engineering division. Wherever they are based in the world, each local unit would report to its 'product' division.

4 *Functional structure.* The organisation structure in which each function reports through its line managers to the functional director at the top of the organisation. For HR that would mean that each location would report to a regional HR manager and ultimately to the HR director.

5 *Matrix structure.* Involves more than one reporting relationship in responsibility structures (known as **matrix organisation** in a domestic context). In civil engineering a major company might have a number of projects active around the world at any one time. They will have engineers in each location looking after the project and working with the main contractor. They also have an additional reporting relationship to their line manager in head office.

6 *Holding company structure.* A number of separate companies within the group that are responsible for their own profitability and success. They have a high degree of autonomy over internal activity (including HR) with headquarters acting primarily as financier.

Think about it?

Identify the relative strengths and weakness from an HRM perspective of the different organisational structure models indicated above.

Expatriation or localisation?

In any business activity in another country there will be a need to balance local people (with knowledge of local conditions and business practice) with the requirement of the parent company's systems, procedures, ways of working and strategic plans. That is where some form of **expatriation** comes into play. There are a number of choices available to an organisation when it engages in global activity in relation to its staffing requirements including:

- Recruit local personnel and spend time training them in company practices and so on before 'going live' in the new location.
- Use expatriates already within the company to take over key jobs in the new location and recruit local people as necessary to begin operations.

There are different types of expatriation including:

1 *Home country nationals* (same country as the parent company) who transfer to another country to undertake a particular job.

2 *Third country nationals.* Individuals not from the country that the parent group is based in, neither are they from the country that they are currently based in.

3 *International cadre.* A category or level within a company comprising individuals who move between countries and locations as a standard part of their work assignments.

4 *Secondments.* Short-term assignments to provide specific assistance to a particular location.

The use of expatriates can be a complex and expensive process. For example, there are salary, housing, medical, schooling and other benefits to be considered. It can be disruptive to a family to move location, particularly if there is more than one person with a job. Many countries have localisation policies requiring organisations to give precedence to local people in job appointments. There are three main influencing factors that determine the staffing policies of international businesses including:

1 *Company characteristics*:

- Form of ownership of the foreign operation.
- Industry and technology factors.

- Market tendencies.
- Structural arrangements.
- Operating procedures and systems.
- HR policies of the parent group.
- Cost.

2 *Personal characteristics of expatriates*:

- Lifestyle and ambitions.
- Career expectations.
- Qualifications, experience and training.
- Family circumstances.

3 *Host country characteristics*:

- Level of economic development.
- Political system, stability and requirements.
- Immigration and investment policies.
- Availability of appropriate labour.
- Sociocultural setting.
- Location.

Think about it?

Your company (UK based) is opening a manufacturing division in China. You have been asked for advice by your CEO on whether you should use expatriate managers to take charge of the new project or recruit Chinese managers and bring them to work in the UK for one year before going back to China and starting the new operation. What would be your advice and why?

International HRM

International HRM signifies some degree of integration and oversight of individual location HRM activity. For example, an international HR department might run the salary grading system for all senior managers and expatriates, irrespective of location. It might also be responsible for cross-cultural and expatriate training, and ensuring that the application of local employment conditions do not breech international law or offend against standards that the home market general public deem acceptable. International HRM departments would also be heavily involved in plans to achieve localisation requirements in relation to the diminishing use of expatriate labour. International HRM people would be involved in location scouting projects in order to assess the local legislative and employment frameworks that might be expected as part of a feasibility study.

International HRM refers to situations in which organisations needs to manage people across different cultures – a multinational or global enterprise. However, there is also another less frequently discussed aspect of international HRM, that of the multicultural workforce. These days with the relative ease of international relocation; general migration trends (for economic, political and other reasons); and the growth in political groupings such as the European Union it is not uncommon to find employees from many different countries working in the same organisation. That brings with it the need for HRM in what would have been a 'home country' context to be able to adopt an international dimension to HR practice as well as make provision to meet equality and diversity obligations under domestic legislation.

Think about it?

To what extent is it reasonable to suggest that managing a multicultural workforce in a single location is a form of international HRM?

National and organisational culture

There are many models that seek to explain cultural difference between people. Hofstede (1980) is one of the most frequently quoted. He concluded that there were four main factors that explained the differences found in national culture:

1 *Individualism.* Refers to cultures with a heavy emphasis on the individual taking responsibility for themselves and their family as compared to societies with a collective social emphasis.

2 *Power distance.* Reflects situations where those with little power accept the unequal spread of it in society.

3 *Uncertainty avoidance.* Reflects the degree to which a particular culture seeks to manage uncertainty by encouraging risk taking or encouraging an acceptance that it can be minimised through various means.

4 *Masculinity.* This factor reflects the degree to which a society is dominated by masculine tendencies or, by contrast, feminine characteristics.

Think about it?

What other cultural models have been developed over recent years and how do they differ from Hofstede's ideas?

In terms of organisational culture there would appear to be three levels at which it is used:

1 *Perceived culture.* What is usually observed and experienced by those working within it.

2 *Common values.* The beliefs and values that underpin and determine the perceived culture.

3 *Underlying assumptions.* Behind the common values are the underlying assumptions about the world and how it functions.

Schein (1985) suggested six dimensions that reflect the composition of culture within an organisational context:

- Behavioural regularities.
- Dominant values. The beliefs of individuals and groups in the organisation.
- Norms. The general patterns of behaviour that members of a group are expected to follow.
- Rules. Specific instructions about what must be done, when and how.
- Philosophy. The underlying beliefs that people in a particular culture hold about people in general.
- Climate. The physical layout of buildings, management style and so on all help to create the atmosphere or climate within the company.

Think about it?

To what extent is international HRM simply cultural management?

Hodgetts and Luthans (1991) suggest that the main areas of impact of culture on the strategic aspects of HRM are:

* Degree of centralisation in organisational decision making.
* Approach adopted to reward and the approach to performance and collective behaviour.
* Approach to risk taking.
* Degree of formality in business and organisational relationships.
* Level of organisational loyalty.
* Long or short-term orientation to organisational activity and results.

Cross-cultural communications and co-ordination

These two areas are of particular importance in international HRM as they are both significant areas of organisational functioning but are particular susceptible to cultural influence and, hence, misunderstanding.

1 *Communication.* It is frequently said that the UK and USA are countries that share a common heritage but are separated by a common language. The point being that even though both countries have English as a common language it is not exactly the same language. Language is used within a particular frame of reference and used outside of that context the meaning of a particular phrase will be slightly different. That means that whenever language is being used (particularly when translation is required) care is needed to ensure that the understanding the originator intended is achieved.

2 *Co-ordination.* Bartlett and Goshal (1989) suggest that there are three conventional approaches to co-ordination based on the location of the parent company. They are:

* Centralisation. Typically Japanese in which a powerful headquarters retains all major decision-making rights and tight control of local operations.
* Formalisation. Typically American in which control is achieved through the use of systems, policies and procedures that direct the business and its functioning.
* **Socialisation**. Typically European in that a heavy reliance is placed on a small number of skilled and trusted individuals to know the business and its objectives to such a depth that they can be allowed to run subsidiaries without close or formal intervention from the centre.

> **Think about it?**
>
> *How can HR contribute to the development of effective cross-cultural models of communication and co-ordination?*

Possible exam and assignment questions. There are many possible ways in which exam and assignment questions can seek to explore international issues within HRM. The two main ways in which this topic might be found in a question are introduced here: First as a support theme for the main discussion purpose of the question and, secondly, as a theme in its own right. An example of the first type of question might be:

"The demands placed on the most senior managers of multinational organisations requires that they spend a significant part of their early careers in expatriate positions. Discuss this statement."

This is quite a complex question and there are many possible themes that could be brought into the discussion of it. It involves consideration of the training and development of senior managers and high-flyers and any 'special treatment' that might be considered justifiable for such groups. There is an underling assumption that in order to manage multinational organisations it is necessary to have worked in different countries. That is on top of the discussion of expatriation and its different forms. In essence there is no right or wrong answer to this type of question as there are a number of justifiable viewpoints. For a good answer it would be necessary to bring the various aspects of the discussion together and offer some conclusions based on the weight of argument and views of the individual answering the question.

An example of the second type of question might be:

"Outline the HRM implications for each of the forms of international business that might be found."

The answer to this question would begin with the relevant material summarised in this section of the Companion. It is important to recognise that the forms of international business in the question are different to the forms of organisational structure also outlined in this section of the book. If you addressed structure issues rather than business type you would be unlikely to achieve a pass mark as that is not what the question is asking about! Remember that for a good mark you need to be able to show understanding, not just an ability to regurgitate material committed to memory. In this type of question, understanding could be demonstrated by including such features as a discussion of what the different business types are and how each could be expected to have different HR require-ments in relation to strategy and specific HR areas of work. Also a discussion of the requirement on the employer to achieve consistency in the application of company policy while abiding by local employment legislation requirements and norms should be brought into the discussion. It is the quality of the discussion that would determine the marks awarded in such questions.

Textbook Guide

ARMSTRONG: *Chapter 6.*

BEARDWELL, CLAYDON AND BEARDWELL: *Chapters 15, 16 and 17.*

BLOISI: *Limited reference to this topic across various chapters.*

FOOT AND HOOK: *Limited reference to this topic across various chapters.*

LEOPOLD, HARRIS AND WATSON: *Chapter 10.*

MARCHINGTON AND WILKINSON: *Chapter 1.*

PILBEAM AND CORBRIDGE: *Limited reference to this topic across various chapters.*

REDMAN AND WILKINSON: *Chapters 9 and 10.*

TORRINGTON, HALL AND TAYLOR: *Chapter 30.*

part three

study, writing and revision skills*

If you work through this material you should be better equipped to profit from your lectures and seminars; construct your essays efficiently; develop effective revision strategies and deal with exams more effectively. The overall aim is to provide you with the toolkit that will help you to excel in your studies.

*in collaboration with David McIlroy

3.1	
how to get the most out of your lectures	

Use of lecture notes

Before you go into each lecture you should briefly remind yourself of where it fits into the overall content of both the entire study programme and each topic within it. The more familiar you become with the context, the greater will be your confidence that you understand the lecture and related study material.

It is always beneficial to do some preliminary reading before you enter a lecture. If lecture notes are provided in advance (for example, electronically), then print these out, read over them and take them with you to the lecture. If notes are provided, supplement these with your own notes as you listen. Remember it is easier to learn material the second time round and your notes will greatly facilitate that process.

Mastering technical terms

Let us assume that in an early lecture you are introduced to a series of new terms. This can be threatening, especially if you have to face a string of them in one lecture. The uncertainty about them may impair your ability to benefit fully from the lecture.

In terms of learning new words, it will be very useful if you can first try to work out what they mean from their context as well as using a glossary of terms. It would also be very useful if you could obtain a small indexed notebook and use this to build up your own glossary of terms.

Checklist for mastering terms used in your lectures

✓ Read lecture notes before the lectures and list any unfamiliar terms.
✓ Read over the listed terms until you are familiar with their sound.
✓ Try to work out meanings of terms from their context.

✓ Write out a sentence that includes the new word (do this for each word).
✓ Meet with other students and test each other with the technical terms.
✓ Jot down new words you hear in lectures and check out the meaning soon afterwards.

> *Your confidence will increase when you begin to follow discussions that contain technical terms, and more so when you can use the terms in speaking and writing.*

Developing independent study

If you adopt effective independent learning strategies you will improve your personal academic performance. The issues raised in lectures are pointers to provide direction and structure for your extended personal pursuit of the relevant literature. Your aim should invariably be to build on what you are given, and you should never concentrate only on the basic material from lectures in an assignment or exam.

> *It is always interesting for a marker to read work that contains recent studies not referred to in lectures or textbooks.*

Note taking strategy

Note taking in lectures will only be perfected through trial and error. What works for one student, does not work for another. Some students can write more quickly than others, some are better at shorthand and some are better at deciphering their own scrawl! The problem will always be to try to find a balance between concentrating on what you hear and making sufficient notes to enable you to comprehend later what you have heard.

Guidelines for note taking in lectures

• Develop the note taking strategy that works best for you.
• Work at finding a balance between listening and writing.
• Make use of shorthand (for example, a few key words may summarise a story).

- Too much writing may impair the flow of the lecture for you and the quality of your notes.
- Limited notes are better than none.
- It is essential to 'tidy up' notes as soon as possible after a lecture.
- Reading over notes soon after lectures will consolidate your learning.

Developing the lecture

Some lecturers introduce ways of making lectures more interactive. For example, asking questions in a lecture. A list of suggestions is presented below to help you take the initiative in developing lecture content.

Checklist to ensure that the lecture is not merely a passive experience

✓ Highlight points that you would like to develop in personal study.

✓ Trace connections between the lecture and other parts of your study programme.

✓ Bring together notes from the lecture and other sources.

✓ Restructure the lecture outline into your own preferred format.

✓ Think of ways in which aspects of the lecture material can be applied.

✓ Design ways in which aspects of the lecture material can be illustrated.

✓ If the lecturer invites questions, make a note of all the questions asked.

✓ Follow up on issues of interest that have arisen out of the lecture.

> *You can contribute to this active involvement in a lecture by engaging with the material before, during and after it is delivered.*

3.2	
how to make the most of seminars	

Not to be underestimated

Interaction between students and lecturers during seminars can considerably enhance the learning and development process.

Checklist – some useful features of seminars

✓ Can identify problems that you had not thought of.
✓ Can clear up confusing issues.
✓ Allow you to ask questions and make comments.
✓ Can help you develop friendships and teamwork.
✓ Enable you to refresh and consolidate your knowledge.
✓ Can help you sharpen motivation and redirect study efforts.

An asset to complement other learning activities

In a seminar you will hear a variety of contributions, and different perspectives and emphases. You will have the chance to interrupt and the experience of being interrupted! You will also learn that you can get things wrong and still survive! It is often the case that when one student admits that they did not know something, other students quickly admit the same. If you can learn to ask questions and not feel stupid, then seminars will give you a learning benefit.

Creating the right climate in seminars

It has been said that we have been given only one mouth to talk, but two ears to listen. One potential problem with seminars is that some students may take a while to learn this. In seminars the challenge is to strike a balance between listening and speaking. It is important to speak, even if it is just to repeat something that you agree with. You can also learn to disagree in an agreeable way. For example, you can raise a question against what someone else has said but pose it in a good way – for instance, 'If that is the case, does that not mean that ...'. In addition it is perfectly possible to disagree with others amicably by avoiding personal attacks.

An opportunity to contribute

If you have never made a contribution to a seminar before, you may need something to use as an 'ice breaker'. It does not matter if your first contribution is only a sentence or two – the important thing is to make a start. One way to do this is to make brief notes as others contribute and, while doing this, a question or two might arise in your mind. If your first contribution is a question, that is a good start. Or it may be that you will be able to point out some connection between what others have said, or identify conflicting opinions that need to be resolved.

EXERCISE

See if you can suggest how you might resolve some of the following problems that might hinder you from making a contribution to seminars.

One student who dominates and monopolises the discussion.

✓..

✓..

Someone else has already said what you really want to say.

✓..

✓..

Fear that someone else will correct you and make you feel stupid.

✓..

✓..

Feel that your contribution might be seen as short and shallow.

✓...

✓...

A previous negative experience puts you off making any more contributions:

✓...

✓...

Strategies for benefiting from your seminar experience

If you are required to bring a presentation to your seminar, you might want to consult the chapter on presentations in a complementary study guide (McIlroy, 2003). See also the summary bullet points below.

If required to give a presentation

- Have a practice before.
- If using visuals, do not obstruct them.
- Check out that all equipment works.
- Space out points clearly on visuals.
- Make sure your talk synchronises with the slide on view.
- Project your voice so that everyone in the room can hear.
- Inflect your voice and do not stand motionless.
- Spread eye contact around the audience.
- Remember it is better to finish a little early than run over time.
- Summarise the main points at the end.

Checklist – how to benefit from seminars

✓ Do some preparatory reading.

✓ Familiarise yourself with the main ideas to be addressed.

✓ Make notes during the seminar.

✓ Make some verbal contribution, even ask a question.

✓ Remind yourself of the skills you can develop.

✓ Trace learning links from the seminar to other topics on your programme.

✓ Make brief bullet points on what you should follow up on.

✓ Read over your notes as soon as possible after the seminar.

✓ Continue discussion with fellow students after the seminar has ended.

3.3	
essay writing tips	

Getting into the flow

In essay writing one of your first aims should be to get your mind active and engaged with your subject. You can 'warm up' for your essay by tossing ideas to and fro in your head before you begin to plan your essay. This will allow you to think within the framework of your topic.

The tributary principle

A tributary is a stream that runs into a main river. Similarly in an essay you should ensure that every idea you introduce is moving toward the overall theme you are addressing. It is one thing to have grasped your subject thoroughly, but quite another to convince your reader that this is the case. Your aim should be to build up ideas sentence-by-sentence and paragraph-by-paragraph, until you have communicated your clear purpose to the reader.

> *It is important in essay writing that you include material which is relevant and that you also make linking statements showing the connections to the reader.*

Listing and linking the key concepts

All subjects will have central concepts that can sometimes be usefully labelled by a single word. Course textbooks may include a glossary of terms and these provide a direct route to the mastery of the topic. Ensure that you learn these words and understand their definitions, and that you can link the key words and ideas together.

EXAMPLE

Write an essay on 'Discuss the major stages in the resourcing process'.

You might decide to draft your outline points in note form or you may prefer to use a mind map approach (see Figure 3.1).

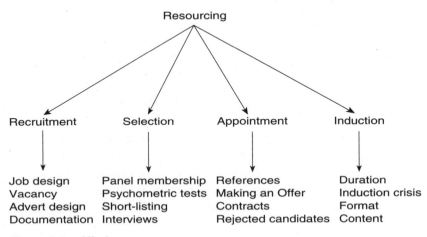

Figure 3.1   Mind map

An adversarial system

In higher education students are required to make the transition from descriptive to critical writing. The critical approach is like a legal case with both a prosecution and a defence to present opposing sides of the argument. Your concern should also be to explore all sides of the argument in an objective, balanced and fair manner. An essay is not a crusade for a cause in which the contrary arguments are not addressed. This means that you should show awareness of the different arguments, and should represent and evaluate these as accurately as possible.

Stirring up passions

The above does not mean that you are not entitled to a personal opinion or to feel passionately about your subject. On the contrary, such feelings may well be an advantage if you can bring them under control and channel them into effective writing. How strongly you feel about a topic or how much you are interested in it may depend on whether you choose the topic or whether it has been given to you.

An issue that may stir up passions: 'The HRM function has nothing to contribute to the profitability of an organisation?'

For

- The HRM function is not a line department.
- HRM practitioners do not have the power to direct human behaviour at work.
- Human behaviour is sometimes uncertain and unpredictable.
- HRM activity costs money and there are not many opportunities to generate income from it.
- Because some HR activity is determined by employment legislation and social/labour market factors the cost of employing labour invariably rises.
- Not many HR practitioners have line management experience and so are not able to relate to the 'people management' needs of line managers.
- It is difficult to measure the actual contribution of HR practitioners to profitability.

Against

- People must be managed irrespective of who is involved.
- HR can enhance line management capabilities in managing people.
- HR could design cost-effective people management schemes.
- Understanding employment legislation and employment rights can minimise legal costs and enhance employee commitment.
- There exists a moral and ethical aspect to the employment of people.
- Effective HR practice can contribute to employee retention and development which reduces cost.
- HR can contribute to effective people management policy and practice, consequently maximising the value of the human capital.

Structuring an outline

Whenever you write on a subject, it is essential that you put this into a structure that will allow your thoughts to be communicated clearly. For example, you might plan for an introduction, a central section containing the substance of the discussion or argument, and a conclusion. The substantive central section may be divided by three main headings, each with several subheadings (see Example below).

> *A good structure will help you to balance the weight of each of your arguments against each other, and arrange your points in the order that will facilitate the fluent progression of your argument.*

EXAMPLE

Discuss the view that effective reward system design can contribute to high performance working.

1   *Introduction*
2   *Reward system design*

- Basic wage/salary structure.
- Pay policy and practice.
- Incentive/benefit arrangements.
- Employee involvement in the process.

3   *High performance working*

- Organisational ability to combine people, technology, management and productivity into sustainable competitive advantage.
- Competitor benchmarking with regard to high performance working.
- Employer philosophy with regard to role of people at work.
- Continuous improvement and measurement of performance.

4   *Reward for high performance*

- Options for pay progression (and promotion) based on delivery of preferred employee behaviours.
- Options for measurement (qualitative or quantitative) of high performance activity.
- Performance management practices targeted at high performance working deliverables.
- Incentive scheme design for rewarding high performance working.
- Other HR options for promoting high performance working.

5   *Conclusions*

Finding major questions

When you are constructing a draft outline for an essay or project, you should ask what major question or questions need to be addressed. It would be useful to make a list of all the issues that spring to mind. If you were asked to write an essay about the effectiveness of the HR department in a particular case study company you might, as your starting point, pose the following questions.

EXAMPLE

The effectiveness of the HR department in the XYZ Company: initial questions.

- Is there an HR department in existence in the company and what is its form and profile?
- How does the HR department interact with management, line departments and trade unions?
- What does 'effectiveness' mean in relation to HR activity?
- What are the norms for HR organisation in similar organisations?
- What does 'best practice' suggest as the way to organise HR activity?
- What evidence is there for effectiveness in HR practice?
- What evidence is there for ineffectiveness in HR practice?
- What evidence is there for manager/employee/HR practitioner views of the HR department's effectiveness?

Rest your case

In exams and essay questions it is assumed (even if not directly specified) that you will use evidence to support your claims. Therefore, when you write your essay you should ensure that it is appropriately sprinkled with relevant evidence and references. By the time the assessor reaches the end of your work, they should be convinced that your conclusions are evidence based.

> *Show that what you have asserted is based on recognised (up-to-date) sources.*
> *Spread your citations across your essay rather than compressing them into a paragraph or two at the beginning and end.*

Careful use of quotations

Although it is desirable to present a good range of cited sources, it is not good practice just to paste together what others have said with no evaluation of their work. It is generally good to avoid very lengthy quotes – short ones can be very effective. Aim at blending the quotations as naturally as possible into the flow of your sentences. Also it is good to vary your practices – sometimes use short, direct, brief quotes in quotation marks (cite page number as well as author and year), and at times summarise the gist of a quote in your own words. In this case you should leave out the quotation marks and page number. Recognise the difference in 'evidence quality' between refereed (or peer reviewed) journals, textbooks, research books, and professional texts and non academic refereed magazines, newspapers, Internet sources, etc.

In terms of referencing there are some general points that contribute to good practice including:

- If a reference is cited in the text, it must be in the list at the end (and vice versa).
- Names and dates in text should correspond exactly with the listing in references or bibliography.
- Lists of references and bibliography should be in alphabetical order by the surname (not the initials) of the author or first author.
- Any reference you make in the text should be traceable by the reader (they should clearly be able to identify, trace and physically examine the source for themselves using the information supplied).

A clearly defined introduction

In an introduction to an essay you have the opportunity to define the problem or issue that is being addressed and to set it within context. Resist the temptation to elaborate on any issue at the introductory stage. The introduction should provide little tasters of what will follow in order to whet the reader's appetite.

If you leave the introduction and definition of your problem until the end of your writing, you will be better placed to map out the directions that will be taken.

Conclusion – adding the finishing touches

In the conclusion you should aim to tie your essay together in a clear and coherent manner. This is your opportunity to identify where the strongest evidence points or where the balance of probability lies. The conclusion to an exam question often has to be written hurriedly under the pressure of time, but with course work you have time to refine the content. It should be your goal to make the conclusion a smooth finish that does justice to the range of content in succinct form.

Checklist – summary for essay writing

- ✓ Before you start – have a 'warm up' by tossing the issues around in your head.
- ✓ List the major concepts and link them in fluent form.
- ✓ Design a structure (outline) that will facilitate balance, progression, fluency and clarity.
- ✓ Pose questions and address these in critical fashion.
- ✓ Demonstrate that your arguments rest on evidence and spread cited sources across your essay.
- ✓ Provide an introduction that sets the scene and a conclusion that rounds off the arguments.

3.4	
revision hints and tips	

The return journey

Revision is a means to 'revisit' what you have encountered before. Familiarity with your material can help reduce anxiety, inspire confidence, and fuel motivation for further learning and good performance.

> *If you are to capitalise on your revision period, then you must have your materials arranged and at hand for the time when you are ready to make your 'return journey' through your notes.*

Start at the beginning

Strategy for revision should be on your mind from your first lecture. Do not waste any lecture, tutorial, seminar, group discussion, and so on by letting the material evaporate into thin air. Get into the habit of making a few points for revision in a notebook after each learning activity. By establishing this regular practice you will find that what you have learnt becomes consolidated in your mind, and you will also be in a better position to 'import' and 'export' material both within and across subjects.

> *If you do this regularly, and do not make the task too tedious, you will be amazed at how much useful summary material you have accumulated when revision time comes.*

Compile summary notes

It would be useful and convenient to have a notebook or cards on which you can write outline summaries that provide you with an overview of your subject. Such practical resources can easily be slipped into your pocket or bag and produced when you are in a queue, on a bus or train. A glance over your notes will consolidate your learning and encourage you to think further about your subject. Therefore it would also be useful to make a note of the questions you would like to think about in greater depth. Your primary task is to get into the habit of constructing outline notes that will be useful for revision, and an example is provided below.

EXAMPLE

The features of non-verbal communication (relevant to employee relations, performance management and training interviews within HRM).

1   *Aspects of non-verbal communication that run parallel with language*:

- Pauses.
- Tone of voice.
- Inflection of voice.
- Speed of voice.

2   *Facets of non-verbal communication related to use of body parts*:

- How close to stand to others.
- How much to use the hands.
- Whether to make physical contact – for example, touching, hugging, handshake.
- Extent and frequency of eye contact.

3   *General features that augment communication*:

- Use of smiles and frowns.
- Use of eyebrows.
- Expressions of boredom or interest.
- Dress and appearance.

Keep organised records

One approach is to keep a folder for each subject and divide this into topics using subject dividers to keep them apart. Make a numbered list of the contents at the beginning of the folder and list each topic clearly. Notes may come from lectures, seminars, tutorials, Internet searches, personal notes, etc. It is also essential that when you remove these for consultation you return them to their 'home' immediately after use.

Academic success has as much to do with good organisation and planning, as it has to do with ability. The value of the quality material you have accumulated during your academic programme may be diminished because you have not organised it into an easily retrievable form.

Use past papers

Revision will be very limited if it is confined to memory work. You should by all means read over your revision cards or notebook. However, it is also essential that you become familiar with previous exam papers so that you will have some idea of how the questions are likely to be framed. Therefore, build up a good range of past exam papers and add these to your folder.

EXAMPLE

Evaluate the advantages and disadvantages of recognising a trade union with collective bargaining rights for all non-managerial level employees in large national supermarket.

Immediately you can see that you will require two lists, as below.

Advantages

- Single body to negotiate pay levels with.
- Eliminates need to deal with thousands of individual employees over terms and conditions of employment.
- Contributes to employees feeling recognised as a significant resource within the business.
- Contributes to higher standards of people management among line managers.
- Prevents fragmentation of employee representation arrangements.
- Can encourage consistency in matters such as discipline, health and safety, and other welfare arrangements.
- Can encourage a partnership approach to work within the organisation.

Disadvantages

- Introduces a third party to organisational affairs.
- Provides a body that can 'stand-up' to management on behalf of employees.
- Not all employees may want to be members of the union.
- Some union officials may seek to undermine management.
- Cost implications of allowing time off and other rights of union representatives.
- Union activity could divert employee attention away from management's agenda.

You will have also noticed the word 'evaluate' in the question – so you must make judgements. You may decide to work through advantages first and then through disadvantages, or you may prefer to compare point by point as you go along. Whatever conclusion you come to may be down to personal subjective preference, but at least you will have worked through all the issues from both standpoints. Ensure that your revision includes critical thinking as well as memory work.

Employ effective mnemonics (memory aids)

Mnemonics can be simply defined as aids to memory – devices that will help you recall information that might otherwise be difficult to retrieve from memory. For example, if you find an old toy in the attic of your house it may suddenly trigger a flood of childhood memories associated with it. Mnemonics can, therefore, be thought of as keys that open the memory's storehouse.

The Location Method

This technique is where a familiar journey is used to 'place' the facts that you wish to remember at various landmarks along the route – for example, a bus stop, a car park, a shop, a store, a bend, a police station, a traffic light and so on. This has the advantage of making an association of the information you have to learn with other material that is already firmly embedded and structured in your memory.

Visualisation

Turn information into pictures – for instance, the worked example given above about the advantages and disadvantages of trade union recognition could be envisaged as two tug-of-war teams that pull against each other. You could, for example, visualise each player as an argument and have the label written on their T-shirt.

Alliteration

Find a series of words that all begin with the same letter as the target.

Peg system

'Hang' information on to a term so that when you hear the term you will remember the ideas connected with it.

Hierarchical system

This is a development of the previous point with higher order, middle order and lower order terms. For example, you could think of the continents of the world (higher order), and then group these into the countries under them (middle order). Under countries you could have cities, rivers and mountains (lower order).

Acronyms

Take the first letter of all the key words and make a word. For example, objectives should be SMART – Specific, Measurable, Attainable, Realistic, Time-bounded.

Mind maps

These encourage you to draw lines that stretch out from the central idea to subsidiary ideas and, in turn, to develop subsidiary ideas in the same way. The method has the advantage of giving you the complete picture at a glance, although they can become a complex work of art!

Rhymes and chimes

These are words that rhyme and words that end with a similar sound (for example, commemoration, celebration, anticipation).

Alternate between methods

You should work at finding a balance between the two revision methods – memory and reading. Outline revision cards might be best reserved for short bus journeys, whereas extended reading might be better employed for longer revision slots at home or in the library. However, remember that it is not sufficient to present outline points in response to an exam question (although it is better to do this than nothing if you have run out of time). Your aim should be to add substance, evidence and arguments to your basic points.

In revision it is useful to alternate between scanning over your outline points, and reading through your notes, articles, chapters, and so on in an in-depth manner. Also, the use of different times, places and methods will provide you with the variety that might prevent monotony.

Imagine a course on human resource management.
Your major outline topics might include:

- Managing people in a social context.
- The legal context of HRM.
- HR planning, resourcing and retention.
- Training and development.
- Performance and behaviour management.
- Reward management.
- Employee relations.
- Health and safety at work.
- Equality and diversity.
- Strategy and HRM.
- International HRM.

This outline would be your overall, bird's eye view of the course. You could then add all the relevant key terms under each heading. For example, under reward management you might have listed: job evaluation, grading, broadbanding salary structures, incentive schemes, pay progression and salary surveys. In order to move from memory to understanding you would need to consider the way that the components of a reward system (memory) fitted together into a workable and cohesive part of an organisation's HRM policy and practice (understanding).

> *If you alternate between memory work and reading, you will soon be able to think through the processes by just looking at your outlines.*

Revising with others

If you can find a few other students to revise with, this will provide another approach to your learning. First ensure that others carry their share of the workload and are not merely using your hard work as a shortcut to success! This collective approach would allow you to assess your strengths and weaknesses, and to benefit from the resources and insights of others. Before you meet up you can each design some questions for the whole group to address. The group could also go through past exam papers and discuss the points that might provide an effective response to each question. It should not be the aim of the group to provide standard and identical answers for each group member to mimic.

Checklist – good study habits for revision time

✓ Set a date for the beginning of revision and prepare for 'revision mode'.

✓ Do not force cramming by leaving revision too late.

✓ Take breaks from revision to avoid saturation.

✓ Indulge in relaxing activities to give your mind a break from pressure.

✓ Minimise or eliminate the use of alcohol during the revision season.

✓ Get into a good rhythm of sleep to allow renewal of your mind.

✓ Avoid excessive caffeine, especially at night, so that sleep is not disrupted.

✓ Try to adhere to regular eating patterns.

✓ Try to have a brisk walk in fresh air each day (for example, in the park).

✓ Avoid excessive dependence on junk food and snacks.

3.5	
exam tips	

Handling your nerves

Exam nerves are not unusual and it has been concluded that test anxiety arises because of the perception that your performance is being evaluated, that the consequences are likely to be serious and that you are working under the pressure of a time restriction. However, if you focus on the task at hand rather than on feeding a downward negative spiral in your thinking patterns, this will help you to keep your nerves under control. In the run-up to you exams you can practice some simple relaxation techniques that will help you to bring stress under control.

Practices that may help reduce or buffer the effects of exam stress

- Listening to music.
- Going for a brisk walk.
- Simple breathing exercises.
- Some muscle relaxation.
- Watching a movie.
- Enjoying some laughter.
- Doing some exercise.
- Relaxing in a bath (with music if preferred).

The most appropriate practice is going to be the one (or combination) that works for you – perhaps best discovered through trial and error. Some of the above techniques can be practised on the morning of the exam, and even the memory of them can be used just before the exam. For example, you could run over a relaxing tune in your head, and have this echo inside you as you enter the exam room. The idea behind all this is, first, stress levels come down, and second, relaxing thoughts will displace stressful reactions.

> *It is important you are convinced that your stress levels can be brought under control – and that you can have a say in this. Do not give anxiety a vacuum to work in.*

Time management

The all-important matter as you approach an exam is to develop the belief that you can take control of the situation. One of the issues you will need to be clear about before the exam is the length of time you should allocate to each question. Sometimes this can be quite simple (although it is always necessary to read the rubric carefully) – for example, if two questions are to be answered in a two-hour paper, you should allow one hour for each question. If it is a two-hour paper with one essay question and 5 shorter answers, you could allow one hour for the essay and 12 minutes each for the shorter questions. However, you always need to check out the questions' weighting – that is, how many marks are allocated to each question. You will also need to deduct what-ever time it takes you to read over the paper and to choose your questions. It is important to give yourself some practice on the papers you are likely to face.

Remember to check that the structure of your exam paper is the same as in previous years, and do not forget that excessive time spent on your 'strongest' question may not compensate for very poor, rushed answers to other questions. Also ensure that you read the rubric carefully in the exam.

EXERCISE

Examples for working out the division of exam labour by time

1 A three-hour paper with four compulsory questions (equally weighted in marks).

2 A three-hour paper with two essays and ten short questions (each of the three 'sections' carry one-third of the marks).

3 A two-hour paper with two essay questions and 100 multiple-choice questions (half of the marks are allocated to the two essays and half of the marks are attached to the multiple choice section).

Get into the calculating frame of mind and be sure to have the calculations done before the exam. Ensure that the structure of the exam has not changed since the last one. Also deduct the time taken to read over the paper in allocating time to each question.

Suggested answers to previous exercise

1 This allows 45 minutes for each question (4 questions × 45 minutes = 2 hours). However, if you allow 40 minutes for each question this will give you 20 minutes (4 questions × 5 minutes) to read over the paper and plan your outlines.

2 This allows 1 hour on each of the 2 major questions, and 1 hour on the 10 short questions. For the 2 major questions you could allow 10 minutes for reading and planning on each, and 50 minutes for writing. In the 10 short questions, you could allow 6 minutes in total for each (10 questions × 6 minutes = 60 minutes). However, if you allow approximately 1 minute reading and planning time, this will allow 5 minutes writing time for each question.

3   Divide 120 minutes by 3 questions – which allows 40 minutes for each. You could, for example, allow 5 minutes reading/planning time for each essay and 35 minutes for writing (or 10 minutes reading/planning and 30 minutes for writing). After you have completed the 2 major questions, you are left with 40 minutes to tackle the 100 multiple-choice questions.

Task management

Some students prefer to plan all outlines and draft work at the beginning, while others prefer to plan one answer and finish writing it before proceeding to the next question. Decide on your strategy before you enter the exam room and stick to your plan. When you have done your draft, you should allow the appropriate time for writing each answer – and stick to it! This will prevent you from excessive treatment of some questions while falling short on others.

> *Keep aware of time limitations as this will help you to write succinctly, keep focused on the task and prevent you dressing up your responses with unnecessary padding.*

Attend to practical details

There are always students who turn up late, or go to the wrong venue, or arrive for the wrong exam, or do not turn up at all! Check and re-check that you have all the details of each exam correctly noted. What you don't need is to arrive late and then have to tame your panic reactions. The exam season is the time when you should aim to be at your best.

Make note of the following details and check that you have taken control of each one.

Checklist – practical exam details

✓ Check that you have the correct venue.
✓ Make sure you know how to locate the venue before the exam day.
✓ Ensure that the exam time you have noted is accurate.
✓ Allow sufficient time for your journey and consider the possibility of delays.
✓ Bring an adequate supply of stationery, pens, etc. and include back up.
✓ Bring a watch for your time and task management.

✓ You may need some liquid such as a small bottle of still water.

✓ You may also need to bring some tissues.

✓ Make sure you have your student card or other required proof of identity.

✓ Observe whatever exam regulations your university/college has set in place.

✓ Fill in required personal details before the exam begins.

✓ Go to the toilet before the exam begins!

Control wandering thoughts

Students who frequently lift their heads and look away from their scripts during exams tend to perform poorly. The implication is that such students are taking too much time out when they should be on task. The distracting thoughts may be either related to the exam itself or totally irrelevant to it. The net effect in both cases is to distract you from the task at hand and reduce your performance.

> *One way to fail your exam is to get up and walk out of the room, but another way is to 'leave' the room mentally by being preoccupied with distracting thoughts.*

Practical suggestions for controlling wandering thoughts

• Be aware that this problem is detrimental to performance.
• Do not look around to find distractions.
• If distracted, write down 'keep focused on task'.
• If distracted again, look back at above and continue to do this.
• Start to draft rough work as soon as you can.
• If you struggle with initial focus then re-read or elaborate on your rough work.
• If you have commenced your essay, re-read your last paragraph (or two).
• Do not throw fuel on your distracting thoughts – starve them by re-engaging with the task at hand.

Art of 'name dropping'

In most topics at university you will be required to cite studies as evidence for your arguments and to link these to the names of researchers, scholars or theorists. It will help if you can use the correct dates or at least the decades, and it is good to demonstrate that you have used contemporary sources and have done some independent work. A marker will have dozens if not hundreds of scripts to work through and they will know if you are just repeating the same phrases from the same sources as everyone else. There is inevitably a certain amount of this that must go on, but there is room for you to add fresh and original touches that demonstrate independence and imagination.

Give the clear impression that you have done more than the bare minimum and that you have enthusiasm for the subject. Also, spread the use of researchers' names across your exam essay rather than compressing them into the first and last paragraphs.

Flight, freeze or fight

The autonomic nervous system(ANS) is activated when danger or apparent danger is imminent. Of course the threat does not have to be physical, as in the case of an exam. Symptoms may include deep breathing, trembling, headaches, nausea, tension, dry mouth and palpitations. How should we react to these once they have been triggered? To run away is one possible response – flight. A second possible response is to freeze on the spot. The third option, to fight back, would be more productive in an exam. That means to 'tackle' the questions and not to run away from the challenge before you.

Rising to the challenge

The following list offers suggestions for how you might take control in an exam:

- Enter the exam room with all the points you will need to use.
- Choose the exam questions.
- Prepare your time management.
- Keep focused on the task at hand and do not become sidetracked.
- Match your points to the appropriate question.
- Do not be content with the minimum standard such as a mere pass.
- Do not be content with preparing one or two strong points.
- Choose relevant points and support with evidence.
- Do not dress up your essay with unnecessary padding.

3.6	
tips on interpreting essay and exam questions	

When we encounter things for the first time the tendency is to impose the nearest similar and familiar template onto what we think we see. The same can also apply to exam or essay questions. You are required to 'answer the question as set' but you may incorrectly interpret the question. This is especially likely if you have primed yourself to expect certain questions to appear. Although examiners do not deliberately design questions to catch you out, they cannot prevent you from reading things into them that were not intended.

The most important rule to remember in an exam or writing an essay is that you must answer the question as set and not a question that you had hoped for!

EXAMPLE

Discuss some of the strategies that might be used by an organisation for increasing the number of people responding to adverts for job vacancies which it places in national newspapers.

Directly relevant points:

- Company reputation.
- Advert size, design and content.
- Appropriateness of job vacancy to newspaper readership.
- Terms and conditions of employment offered.
- Ease of application process.
- Labour market conditions.
- Day of week advertised.

Less relevant points:

- Type of interview to be used.
- Date of interviews.
- Structure of the organisation.
- Requirement for medical screening and references for successful appointment.
- Induction arrangements.
- Cost of advertising space.
- Relevant advantages offered by the use of recruitment consultants.

Although some of the points listed in the 'less relevant' category may be relevant to recruitment overall, they are not directly relevant to an answer which seeks to explore how to increase the level of response to jobs advertised through the national press. If the question had sought an answer which focussed on improving the resourcing process over-all, then some of those points would have been relevant. However, some of the points could be mentioned briefly without going off at a tangent.

Resist including the wealth of fascinating material at your disposal that is not directly relevant to answering the question as set.

Missing your question

Students should always revise enough topics to avoid selling them-selves short in the exam – the sport of 'question spotting' is always a risky game to play. However, the reality could be that an expected question might be there, but not immediately obvious. Expecting questions to be worded in certain ways can lead to them being missed if they are couched in different ways, especially when scanned quickly.

Always read over questions carefully, slowly and thoughtfully.

Pursue a critical approach

In degree courses you are expected to evaluate and to write critically rather than to simply describe ideas, theories or models. However, it will be necessary to use some minimal description of models or theory as the raw material for your debate. The discussion in Section 4 above in relation to the evaluation of union recognition in a national supermarket is very relevant here and should be re-read.

Analyse the parts

An effective essay cannot be constructed without reference to the sub-parts associated with the argument. The identification of the parts will arise as you break down the question into the themes that it suggests to you. Although the breaking down of a question into components is not sufficient for an excellent essay, it is a necessary starting point.

> To achieve a good response to an exam or essay question, aim to integrate all the individual issues presented in a manner that gives shape and direction to your efforts.

EXAMPLE

Discuss whether disciplinary warnings should be left permanently on an employee's record or whether they should be removed automatically after a maximum period of one year.

Two parts to this question are clearly suggested – permanence or removal after one year, and you would need to do justice to each in your answer. Other issues that arise in relation to these are left for you to suggest and discuss. Examples might be fairness, nature of the disciplinary offences, legal requirement, company practice, disciplinary policy and subsequent employee behaviour.

> Get into the habit of 'stepping sideways' and looking at questions from several angles. The best way to do this is by practice, for example on previous exam papers.

Checklist – ensuring that questions are understood before being fully addressed

✓ Read over the chosen question several times.

✓ Write it down to ensure that it is clear.

✓ Check that you have not omitted any important aspect or point of emphasis.

✓ Ensure that you do not wrongly impose preconceived expectations on the question.

✓ Break the question into parts (dismantle and rebuild).

When asked to discuss or critique

Students often ask how much of their own opinion they should include in an essay. In a discussion, when you raise one issue, another one can arise out of it. In a discussion or critique your aim should be not just to identify and define all the parts that contribute, but also to show where they fit (or don't fit) into the overall picture. It would be the aim to discuss and critique or evaluate the range of arguments and perspectives (including those issues that appear to be inconclusive) in order to arrive at some reasoned conclusions.

> Although the word 'discuss' implies some allowance for your opinion, remember that this should be informed opinion rather than groundless speculation. Also, there must be direction, order, structure and an end product.

Checklist – features of a response to a 'discuss' question

✓ Contains a chain of issues that lead into each other in sequence.

✓ Clear shape and direction is unfolded in the progression of the argument.

✓ Underpinned by reference to findings and certainties.

✓ Identification of issues where doubt remains.

✓ Tone of argument may be tentative but should not be vague.

If asked to compare and contrast

When asked to compare and contrast, you should be thinking in terms of similarities and differences. You should ask what the two issues share in common, and what features of each are distinct. Your preferred strategy for tackling this might be to work first through all the similarities and then through all the contrasts (or vice versa). On the other hand, you might prefer to work through a similarity and contrast, followed by another similarity and contrast, and so on.

Whenever evaluation is requested

When asked to evaluate some theory or concept in your own academic field of study you are being invited to weigh-up the value or contribution of the central issue. That implies that you have some point of comparison (perhaps between competing ideas, models or theories), or that you have other evidence on which to call to support a conclusion about the central issue. Some summary points to guide you in seeking to evaluate are presented below:

- Has the theory/concept stood the test of time?
- Is there a supportive evidence base that would not easily be overturned?
- Are there questionable elements that have been or should be challenged?
- Does more recent evidence point to a need for modification?
- Is the theory/concept robust and likely to be around for the foreseeable future?
- Could it be strengthened through being merged with other theories/concepts?

It should now be clear that learning should not merely be a mechanical exercise, such as just memorising and reproducing study material. Quality learning also involves making connections between ideas, thinking at a deeper level by attempting to understand your material and developing a critical approach to learning.

glossary	

ACAS
The Advisory, Conciliation and Arbitration Service. Independent body charged with seeking to improve employee relations and resolve disputes between employers and employees.

Action learning
A form of learning based on groups seeking to solve real problems.

Affinity benefits
A range of items such as reduced price medical cover, insurance, retail discounts and so on provided to employees at a discounted price by a third party.

Analytical job evaluation
Methods that create a job worth hierarchy, using scores on a range of factors to assess the relative magnitude of each job. Examples include points ranking and a range of proprietary schemes developed by consultancies.

Appraisal – 360-degree
A performance appraisal process whereby an individual is rated on their performance by subordinates, peers, superiors, customers and clients. The individual usually also completes a self-evaluation for use in the process.

Assessment centre
A group recruitment or development process using a series of tests, interviews, group and individual exercises that are scored by a team of assessors in order to evaluate the candidates.

Attitude
A predisposed feeling, thought or behavioural response to a particular stimulus. Acquired through socialisation, education, training and previous experience.

Attrition

A term used to describe the number of employees who have left, had their employment terminated, been made redundant, died, or retired during a specified period of time.

Autonomous work group

A work team with delegated responsibility for a defined part of an organisation's activities with the freedom to organise its own resources, pace of work and allocation of responsibilities.

Balanced business scorecard

A model which enables organisations to translate their vision and strategy into action by measuring results in four areas: financial performance, customer knowledge, internal business processes, and learning and growth.

Base pay (or basic rate or base rate)

The hourly rate or monthly salary paid for a job performed. Does not include shift premiums, benefits, overtime, incentive payments, etc.

Behavioural based interview

A technique which focuses on a candidate's past experiences, behaviours, knowledge, skills and abilities by asking for specific examples of when they were demonstrated. A means of predicting future behaviour and performance.

Benchmark job

A standard job used to make job evaluation decisions or pay comparisons, either within the organisation or a comparable job outside the organisation.

Benefits

A package of additions to the basic wage or salary. Can include car, fuel, pension, holidays, child and/or elder care, health insurance, life insurance, disability insurance, etc.

Broadbanding

A pay strategy that consolidates a large number of relatively narrow pay grades into fewer but broad-banded salary ranges.

Bullying and harassment

The act of intimidating or seeking to force someone to do (or not to do) something by subjecting them to persecution or intimidation.

Bureaucratic

An approach to organising the activities within an organisation which involves specialisation of task, hierarchy, authority and decision making.

Burnout

A feeling of helplessness and of being unable to continue, experienced by some individuals after prolonged exposure to stress.

Cafeteria or flexible benefits

An approach to employee benefits that allows individuals to select specific benefits from the total range available, up to a set limit.

Career progression or ladder

A series of defined levels within a work area (for example, HRM, finance, engineering, marketing) where the levels represent typical requirements for career growth. Parallel ladders and overlapping ladders allow transition from one field to another (for example, from engineering to management). Sometimes called career pathing.

Central Arbitration Committee (CAC)

A national body to which unions can apply if they cannot achieve recognition by an employer. The CAC will seek to facilitate recognition, but failing that can require an employer to recognise a union if evidence exists that a majority of employees wish them to do so.

Collective bargaining

The process by which an employer will negotiate the terms and conditions of employment for a particular group or category of employees with a trade union or other employee representative body.

Commitment	This involves the employee internalising the underlying values and norms held by management, and in so doing committing themselves to management's aims and objectives.
Communication	A process of sharing information and creating relationships in environments designed for directed, goal-oriented behaviour.
Competency	The job behaviours which contribute to individual, team and organisational performance and success.
Competency-based pay	A compensation system that rewards employees for the depth, breadth, and types of behaviours and skills they apply in their work. Sometimes referred to as skill-based and knowledge-based pay.
Competitive advantage	The means of an organisation achieving an advantage over its competitors. People are a major source of competitive advantage; other aspects of an organisation can be replicated but not the people!
Compliance	Following the rules precisely, paying only 'lip service' to the aims and objectives determined by management.
Confidentiality agreement	An agreement (or contract term) restricting the disclosure confidential or proprietary information.
Constructive dismissal	The employee resigns from the organisation but claims that they were forced into doing so by the direct or indirect actions of the employer.
Consultation	A process in which the views and opinions of employees and trade unions are sought before a decision is made by management.
Continuous improvement	A continuous approach adopting incremental and frequent changes to improve operational effectiveness – a journey without end.

Contract for services   The basis of the working arrangement between an independent contractor and an employer which does not grant the status or rights of an employee.

Contract of service   The basis of the working arrangement between an employee and an employer.

Counselling   Helps the 'client' resolve problems by focussing on problem solving and setting goals.

Curriculum vitae (CV)   A written description of work experience, educational background, and skills.

Data protection   The rights of individuals (including employees) in relation to the information held about them by organisations, how it is protected, and the uses to which it can be put.

Delayed appointment   Delaying the start date by a defined period for new staff who have been offered a job but not yet started work following a crisis and the need to cut staff.

Delayering   Achieving a reduction in the total number of people and/or a flatter organisation by the elimination of levels (often managerial/supervisory layers) in the hierarchy.

Direct discrimination   Occurs when an employer bases a decision on factors such as sex or race.

Disciplinary procedure   A procedure aimed at dealing with situations in which an employee behaves contrary to rules of the organisation or their terms of employment.

Discrimination   The favouring of an individual or group to the detriment of others.

Distance learning   Delivering training to individuals and groups in their own environments and at a flexible time through the use of technology, multimedia communications and specially developed study guides.

Diversity

Seeks to ensure that organisations are able to capture the benefits of 'difference' as a means of developing competitive advantage.

Employee assistance programme

A scheme provided through a specialist consultancy to offer support to employees (usually by discussion with a support worker) who experience problems affecting their work.

Employee development

A process involving training and development aimed at maximising the contribution of an employee to the business.

Employee empowerment

Authorisation of an individual to take decisions and action beyond the requirements of their normal job function without the need to obtain specific approval.

Employee involvement

An opportunity for employees to become involved in decision making and/or the running of the business beyond the normal scope of their job.

Employee relations

Refers to the design, implementation and ongoing management of activities related to the development, maintenance, and improvement of relationships between employer and employee.

Employment legislation

The legal aspects associated with employment. Covers issues including equality, termination of employment, consultation, recognition of trade unions, health and safety, discrimination, minimum wage, and so on.

Employment Tribunal	A three-person panel convened to hear matters covered by employment law – for example, unfair dismissal, discrimination, equal pay, etc.
Equality	A legislative-based approach to ensure that disadvantaged groups are not discriminated against in employment matters.
Exit interview	An interview carried out when an employee has resigned to ascertain the reasons why.
Expatriation	There are different forms if expatriation including home country nationals who transfer to another country; third country nationals from neither the home or host country; an international cadre; and secondments.
Extrinsic rewards	Work-related rewards that are not part of the job itself–perhaps an incentive payment – as opposed to intrinsic rewards, such as satisfaction in a job well done.
Felt fair	Used within reward management and employee relations to mean that something should be 'felt to be fair' by the people subjected to the system or procedure if subsequent problems are to be avoided.
FIFO	In redundancy the system of 'first in first out' is one method of choosing those to be released.
Financial assistance (benefits)	Includes mortgage assistance payments; company loans; relocation expenses; season ticket loans; and fees to professional bodies.
Financial participation	Giving employees a financial stake in the success of the business through profit sharing or share options.

Fixed-term contract

An employment contract with a specified end date.

Flexibility

There are various forms of flexibility: numerical (vary the numbers employed depending on work volume); functional (vary the jobs done by employees so that they can move between jobs depending on workload variations); temporal (change the times/periods of work over the day/week/month/year to match seasonal patterns); financial (vary the wage levels to match business activity); and locational (moving locations to meet variable demand for labour). As the flexible firm, it also relates to a specific organisational model which includes core employees and various forms of peripheral employee.

Go slow

A form of industrial action that involves doing less work than would usually be expected or less than the norm.

Grievance

A formal complaint brought by an employee against some aspect of their treatment at work.

Gross misconduct

An act committed by any employee that, if proven, would result in dismissal without notice.

High performance organisation

An organisation in which the combination of people, technology, management and productivity are effectively integrated to provide competitive advantage on a sustainable basis.

HRM (Human Resource Management)

An approach to the management of people that represents a more managerial, strategic activity than personnel management.

Human capital

The 'value' of the collective knowledge, skills, experience and abilities of an organisation's employees. A way of describing peolple which emphasises their financial value to an organisation as resources which need to be acquired and maintained.

Human relations movement

The school of management thinking that originated from the work of Elton Mayo, in which the significance of social groups and processes were emphasized.

Human resource planning

The process of seeking to match present and future human availability to the needs of the organisation.

Incentive schemes

Schemes designed to reward the delivery of specific outcomes at an individual, group, and/or company level.

Incremental pay progression

Progression (usually annually) through the steps in a pay band – pay usually based on service rather than performance.

Indirect discrimination

Occurs when a 'requirement or condition' for a job indirectly disadvantages a particular category of people.

Induction

The process of introducing a new employee into the organisation.

Industrial action

The actions taken by either management or employees to force the other party to accept what the party taking action wants. Can involve strikes, lockouts, go slow actions, overtime/flexibility restrictions, withdrawal of goodwill, or working to rule.

Instrumental approach to work

An approach to work which is based on a trading approach to relationships and the determination of contribution.

Intrinsic rewards

Rewards that are associated with the job itself, such as the opportunity to perform meaningful work and receive feedback on work results.

Job   The collection of tasks, duties, and responsibilities assigned to a position.

Job analysis   The systematic, formal study of the duties and responsibilities that comprise job content. For example, the range of duties, level of cost controlled, number of subordinates reporting to the postholder, objectives to be achieved, and so on.

Job classification   Job evaluation created by comparing jobs on a 'whole' job basis against predefined grade descriptions (or classifications).

Job description   A summary of a job including its purpose and aim; the resources controlled and the associated working relationships and contacts; the specific range of duties and responsibilities involved; and factors such as the skill, effort and working conditions.

Job design   The principles and processes that determine the way in which a particular collection of tasks is combined into a job.

Job evaluation   A formal process (either analytical or non-analytical) to create a job-worth hierarchy within an organisation.

Job family   A group of jobs in the same area of work (for example, engineering) but requiring different levels of skill, effort, responsibility or working conditions (such as, junior versus senior engineer).

Knowledge management   The management of the knowledge available to the organisation from all sources in such a way as to allow the creation of new knowledge and the sharing of existing knowledge together with the manipulation of that knowledge in such a way as to benefit the organisation and the individuals working within it.

Labour market   A pool of potential labour for particular jobs. There are many labour markets defined by a combination of the following factors: (1) geography (that is, internal, local, regional, national, international); (2) industry; (3) education or qualification; and (4) function or occupation.

Labour turnover   The number of people leaving the organisation for any reason, usually expressed as a percentage of the total number employed.

Learning   The relatively permanent change in behaviour or potential behaviour that results from direct or indirect experience.

Learning organisation   The facilitation of learning for all employees and the constant transformation of the organisation in response to that new knowledge and ability.

LIFO   In redundancy the system of 'last in first out' selects those people with least service for release. It is also the cheapest method for the employer, but it may not select those who want to leave or those who are the weakest performers.

Line manager   Every employee reports to a line manager – their boss.

Lockout   A management refusal to allow workers to enter the company premises or to work.

Market pricing   The technique of creating a job-worth hierarchy based on the 'going rate' for benchmark jobs in the labour market(s) relevant to the organisation.

Matrix organisation   An organisational structure where employees report to more then one manager or supervisor.

Mentoring   A one-to-one process between an outside trainer and an employee, whereby the former will offer informal guidance to the latter.

Midpoint   The salary that represents the middle of a given salary range or pay grade.

Minimum wage

The lowest level of hourly wage rate, which is set by government based on recommendations from the Low Pay Commission.

Motivation

A driving force that encourages an individual to behave in particular ways as they seek to achieve a goal; the willingness or energy with which individuals perform their work.

Multi-union recognition

More than one trade union within the company, each recognised for a specific category of employees and with different recognition agreements in place.

Negotiation

Reflects a process of difference reduction through the forming of agreements between individuals and groups who have mutually dependent needs and desires.

New pay

Recognises the complexity of organisational 'reality' and seeks to shape reward decisions rather than offer specific design principles.

Non analytical job evaluation

Method that creates job-worth hierarchy based on the perceived value of the 'whole job'. Examples include classification, ranking, and slotting.

Objective

A target, intention or aim for organisational, departmental or individual effort over a defined timescale.

Occupational health department

Company department responsible for the many aspects of health and safety at work. Might offer medical screening, emergency treatment and training in relation to health, well-being and fitness.

Organisational culture

A pattern that emerges from the interlocking beliefs, values, behaviours and expectations of all the members of an organisation.

Organisational development (OD)

The systematic application of behavioural science knowledge to the planned development of organisational strategies, structures, and processes for maximising performance.

Organisational justice

If either party becomes dissatisfied with the behaviour of the other in relation to the requirements of the employment contract, then discipline and grievance procedures exist to address them – mechanisms for achieving organisational justice.

Organisational structure

The way in which the departments, functions and sections are arranged to allow the organisation to achieve its business objectives.

Outsourcing

Using an external organisation to provide one or more internal functions.

Paired comparison

Job evaluation technique that compares each job to every other to determine which has a higher value; ultimately a rank ordering of jobs would emerge.

Pay progression

The performance- or service-based mechanisms by which an individual progresses from the lowest rate of pay within a particular grade to the highest rate of pay within that same grade.

Pay survey

The gathering of data on wages and salaries paid by other employers.

Peer appraisal

A performance appraisal strategy whereby an individual's job performance is determined by their peers.

Performance

The level of achievement by an individual, measured against what they would be expected to achieve.

Performance appraisal

A process for the determination of how well an individual employee has performed during a given period of time.

Performance management

The many processes through which managers seek to manage performance levels within the organisation.

Performance planning

A total approach to managing performance involving setting performance objectives for the organisation, departments and individuals; monitoring performance delivery; then acting upon the results achieved.

Peripheral working

Workers in various forms of casual, temporary or sub-contracting forms of employment that do not link them to an organisation in any long-term working arrangements.

Person specifications

A variation of the job description that defines what worker characteristics (that is, the knowledge, skills and abilities) are required to perform the job and for it to be carried out competently.

Personal needs (benefits)

These cover such items as maternity and paternity rights above the legal minimum; leave for personal reasons (paid or unpaid); career counselling; career development and training; the chance to work as part of a team working; the existence of well-designed jobs; and the existence of good/effective management practice; flexible working; childcare nurseries or vouchers, and so on.

Personal security (benefits)

These cover items such as pension; health care; death in service benefit; personal accident; enhanced sick pay; enhanced redundancy pay.

Piecework

A payment for each piece or unit of work produced by an employee.

Points rating method	A job evaluation method in which a range of factors are used to determine the relative value of jobs. Each factor has a scale of measurement based on points that are weighted relative to their importance. Each job is evaluated against each of the factors and points are awarded. These points are added together to determine the total job score for each job.
Positive action	Training, development and other encouragement made available to members of disadvantaged groups to facilitate their promotion and career progression.
Positive discrimination	Where an employer seeks to overcome previous discrimination by giving preference to the group previously disadvantaged.
Premieums	Additional payments to cover such things as overtime working; callout requirements; and when working conditions are much worse than normal.
Principled negotiations	An approach to negotiation based on: separating the people from the problem; focusing on interests, not positions; inventing options for mutual gain; and insisting on objective criteria.
Probationary period	Where the parties to a job offer agree that an employee will serve a trial period of a certain duration at the commencement of their employment.
Productivity	The relationship between inputs and outputs, expressed as either an index reflecting (for example) the organisation's sales for each unit of labour, or an index measuring changes across time.
Promotion	The appointment of an employee to a job in a higher grade in the organisation's job hierarchy.

Psychological contract	The actual nature and boundaries of the relationship between employer and employee prescribed through the unwritten and unstated rights and obligations of both parties.
Psychometric testing	The process of mental measurement through the application of tests that measure aspects of personality or other characteristic such as ability or aptitude.
Quality circle	Small groups of people from the same work area who voluntarily meet on a regular basis to identify, investigate, analyse and solve their own work-related problems.
Recognition	Recognition refers to the type of formal contract between a management and trade union or other employee representative body.
Recruitment	The initial stages in the resourcing process. Involves identifying vacancies, ensuring that appropriate documents exist for the job in question, placing adverts and undertaking initial sift of applications to identify a short-list for interview.
Recruitment agency	A company which identifies and helps to find new employees for clients. May involve any of the following activities: placing adverts, initial sorting of applications, initial interviews, psychometric testing, designing adverts, drawing up short-lists for the client to interview, and so on.
Redundancy	The dismissal of an employee when the job that the employee does is no longer required by the organisation.
Resourcing	The process of bringing into an organisation personnel who will possess the appropriate education, qualifications, skills and experience for the post offered.

Retention

The proportion of employees who stay with an organisation in the long term.

Risk management

For HR this usually refers to the requirement under health and safety legislation to identify the level of risk associated with the activities that take place within the organisation.

Sabbatical

This allows individuals to take a break from the company and their career for a specified period of time.

Salary structure

The structure of job grades and pay ranges established within an organisation.

Secondment

Involves moving individuals to other areas of the organisation, parts of the supply chain, charities or to other organisations facing a shortage of particular skills for a specified period to the benefit of all parties.

Selection

The stage in the resourcing process that involves selecting the successful applicant(s) from the pool of available and suitably qualified people recruited.

Self-managed team

A work team in which the team leader is appointed from within the group by members, not appointed by management.

Service centres (for HR provision)

These can be operated in-house or in partner ship with other organisations. They are usually small in size and offer direct advice and support to line managers and others within the organisation, either by phone or over the Internet.

Shift premium

Extra pay allowances made to employees who work on a shift system if it is considered to disrupt 'normal' life patterns.

Short-time working

A temporary reduction in the normal working hours (or days) of employees because of a downturn in business activity.

Single-table bargaining	A situation in which there are multiple unions recognised within a particular company. A clause in each recognition agreement makes provision for all of the unions to negotiate with management in a single process.
Single-union recognition	This represents a situation in which a company recognises one union for all categories of employee.
Skill	Skill refers to acquired measurable behaviours (for example, autoclave operation).
Skill-based pay	A person-based remuneration system based on the repertoire of jobs an employee can perform rather than the specific job that the employee may be doing at a particular time.
SMART objectives	Refers to objectives that are Specific, Measurable, Attainable, Realistic and Time bounded.
Social benefits	Financial help in time of sickness, old age, or unemployment.
Social engineering	An attempt to create particular attitudes, practices, social structures, or social relationships by a dominant group.
Socialisation	The process of learning how things should be done in a particular context.
Spot-rate pay	All employees in a given job are paid at the same rate instead of being within a pay range.
Stakeholder	An individual or group with some an association or interest in the organisation.
Strategic HRM	The process of aligning human resources more closely to the strategic and operating objectives of the organisation.

Strategic reward	The process of seeking to effectively align reward policy and practice to the HR and business strategies of the organisation.
Stress	The pressure encountered as a result of life experiences that place high levels of physical and/or psychological demand on an individual.
Strike	A form of industrial action that involves a withdrawal of labour by the employees either on a temporary or indefinite basis.
Suspension	Usually with pay during a disciplinary investigation when it is deemed to be prejudicial to the investigation for the individual(s) to remain at work. Can be used as a form of disciplinary action (without pay) for a specified period of time as an alternative to dismissal but only if the contract of employment provides for it (or the employee agrees to it as an alternative to dismissal).
Tangible rewards	Rewards that can be physically touched or held (such as bonus payments, gift certificates, and so on).
Team	Implies a small, cohesive group that works effectively as a single unit through being focussed on a common task.
Team leader	Person given the task of leading a team, may be appointed by management or elected by team members from among the group.
Team performance	There are different types of team in performance terms - working group; pseudo-team; potential team; real team; and high performance team.
Team roles	A model consisting of nine roles that exist within a group, developed by Belbin. The roles include: plant, resource investigator, implanter and completer.

Team work Teams are involved in many aspects of organi-sational activity – production and service-related activities; functional teams; cross-functional teams; problem-solving teams; and the management team.

Total quality management (TQM) Based on the involvement of everyone in continually improving the quality of the product, service and customer experience.

Total reward The sum of the financial and non-financial value to the employee of all the elements in the employment package (that is, salary, incentives, benefits, recognition, job satisfaction, organisa-tional affiliation, status, autonomy, etc.) and any other intrinsic or extrinsic rewards of the employ-ment exchange that the employee values.

Trade union An organisation that is formed to represent the interests of members (employees) in discus-sion, consultation and negotiation with their employers. Also provides membership services, government lobbying and sponsorship of Members of Parliament (MPs).

Training and development A process dealing primarily with obtaining the knowledge, attitudes and skills needed to carry out an activity, role or task.

Unfair dismissal The act of terminating an employee's employ-ment for a reason that is not one of the 'fair' reasons indicated in legislation – conduct, capa-bility, legal bar, redundancy, retirement or some other substantial reason (SOSR). Or a dismissal that was not carried out in a 'fair manner' to the satisfaction of an Employment Tribunal.

Victimisation Refers to situations in which the employer takes revenge or action against an employee (or group) because they sought (or assisted others) to claim their legal rights particularly in relation to equality.

Voluntary redundancy   Used when seeking to reduce the number of employees through self selection.

Wage band   A pay structure with a maximum and minimum level of pay attached to each grade. Therefore, different people doing the same job could be paid differently.

Wage–work bargain   The subjective employee and employer views as to what represents a fair exchange in terms of the amount of work done for the wages paid.

Work to rule   A form of industrial action that involves following the established rules and procedures to the letter, with no exceptions.

Work-life balance   The balance between work, family, personal and leisure activities.

Working Time Directive   A set of regulations seeking to control the amount and periods of time that an employee is at the employer's disposal and engaged in carrying out their activities or duties.

bibliography

Armstrong, M. (2006) *A Handbook of Human Resource Practice*. 10th Edition. Kogan Page: London.

Bartlett, C.A. and Goshal, S. (1989) *Managing Across Borders*. Random House: London.

Beardwell, I., Claydon, T. and Beardwell, J. (2007) *Human Resource Management: A Contemporary Approach*. 5th Edition. Pearson Education: Harlow.

Becker, B., Huselid, M. and Ulrich, D. (2001) *The HR Scorecard: Linking People, Strategy and Performance*. Harvard Business School Press: Boston.

Beer, M., Spector, B., Lawrence, P.R., Quinn Mills, D. and Walton, R.E. (1984) *Managing Human Assets*. Free Press: New York.

Beer, M., Lawrence, P.R., Quinn Mills, D. and Walton, R.E. (1985) *Human Resource Management: A General Manager's Perspective*. Free Press: Glencoe, IL.

Belbin, M. (1993) *Team Roles at Work*. Butterworth-Heinemann: Oxford.

Bloisi, W. (2007) *An Introduction to Human Resource Management*. McGraw-Hill: Maidenhead.

Boxall, P. and Purcell, J. (2003) *Strategy and Human Resource Management*. Palgrave Macmillan: Basingstoke.

Fisher, R. and Ury, W. (1986) *Getting to Yes; Negotiating Agreement Without Giving In*. Penguin: New York.

Fombrum, C.J., Tichy, N.M. and Devanna, M.A. (eds) (1984) *Strategic Human Resource Management*. John Wiley: New York.

Foot, M. and Hook, C. (2005) *Introducing Human Resource Management*. 4th edition. Pearson Education: Harlow.

Guest, D. (1989) 'Personnel and HRM: Can you tell the difference?', *Personnel Management* (January) CIPD: London.

Hendry, C., Pettigrew, A.M. and Sparrow, P.R. (1989) 'Linking strategic change, competitive performance and human resource management: results of a UK empirical study', in R. Mansfield (ed.) *Frontiers of Management Research*. Routledge: London.

Hodgetts, R.M. and Luthans, F. (1991) *International Management*. McGraw-Hill: New York.

Hofstede, G. (1980) 'Motivation, leadership and organization: do American theories apply abroad?', *Organizational Dynamics*, Summer: 42–63.

Honey, P. and Mumford, A. (1989) *A Manual of Learning Opportunities*. Peter Honey: Maidenhead.

Jackson, B.W., LaFasto, F., Schultz, H.G. and Kelly, D. (1992) 'Diversity', in B.W. Jackson, F. LaFasto, H.G. Schultz and D. Kelly, *Human Resource Management*, 31(1–2) Spring/summer.

Janis, I.L. (1982) *Victims of Groupthink: A Psychological Study of Foreign Policy, Decisions and Fiascos*. 2nd edition. Houghton and Mifflin: Boston, MA.

Kaplan, R. and Norton, D. (1992) 'The balanced scorecard – measures that drive performance', *Harvard Business Review*, Jan–Feb pp. 77–9.

Kazenbach, J.R. and Smith, D.K. (1993) *The Wisdom of Teams: Creating the High Performance Organization*. Harvard Business School Press: Boston, MA.

LaFasto, F. (1992) 'Baxter healthcare organisation', in B.W. Jackson, F. LaFasto, H.G. Schultz and D. Kelly, *Human Resource Management*, 31, (1–2) Spring/Summer.

Lank, E. (2002) 'Head to head', *People Management*, 8 (4): 46–9.

Legge, K. (2005) *Human Resource Management: Rhetorics and Realities*. Anniversary Edition. Palgrave Macmillan: Basingstoke.

Leopold, J., Harris, L. and Watson, T. (2004) *The Strategic Managing of Human Resources*. Pearson Education: Harlow.

Marchington, M. and Wilkinson, A. (2005) *Human Resource Management at Work*. 3rd Edition. CIPD: London.

Martin, J. (2005) *Organizational Behaviour and Management*. 3rd edition. Thomson Learning: London.

McIlroy, D. (2003) *Studying at University: How to be a Successful Student*. Sage Publications: London.

Mumford, A. (1989) *Management Development: Strategies for Action*. Institute of Personnel Management: London.

Pilbeam, S. and Corbridge, M. (2006) *People Resourcing: Contemporary HRM in Practice*. 3rd edition. Pearson Education: Harlow.

Redman, T. and Wilkinson, A. (2006) *Contemporary Human Resource Management: Text and Cases*. 2nd edition. Pearson Education: Harlow.

Ross, R. and Schneider, R. (1992) *From Equality to Diversity – A Business Case for Equal Opportunities*. Pitman: London.

Schein, E.H. (1985) *Organizational Culture and Leadership*. Jossey Bass: San Francisco, CA.

Schuler, R.S. and Jackson, S.E. (1987) 'Linking competitive strategies with human resource management practices', *Academy of Management Executive*, 9 (3): 207–19.

Schuler, R.S. and Jackson, S.E. (1996) *Human Resource Management: Positioning for the 21st century*. West Publishing: Minneapolis.

Senge, P. (1990) *The Fifth Discipline*. Doubleday: London.

Storey, J. (1992) *Developments in the Management of Human Resources*. Blackwell: Oxford.

Taylor, S. (1998) 'Emotional Labour and the new workplace', in P. Thompson and C. Warhurst, *Workplaces of the Future*. Macmillan: Basingstoke.

Torrington, D., Hall, L. and Taylor, S. (2005) *Human Resource Management*. 6th edition. Prentice Hall: Harlow.

Watson, T.J. (1986) *Management, Organization and Employment Strategy. New Directions in Theory and Practice*. Routledge & Kegan Paul: London.

de Wit, B. and Meyer, R. (1999) *Strategy Synthesis: Resolving Strategy Paradoxes to Create Competitive Advantage*. Thomson Learning: London.

useful websites

In addition to the web-based material that you should be able to access through your textbook and other resources supplied by your lecturer, there should be a wide range of university library based web support services that you would have access to. You should make full use of these to gain access to a wide range of material in addition to book and journal based literature. In addition, below are a few of the major websites that might be expected to have something of relevance to offer you at various stages in your studies of HRM.

http://www.hrmguide.co.uk/ – range of articles and advice from the UK; other country sites also accessible through this source

http://www.shrm.org/ – American site for the Society for Human Resource Management

http://www.intute.ac.uk/socialsciences/cgi-bin/browse.pl?id=120269 &gateway=% – Site run by the Universities of Birmingham and Bristol (among other institutions) that allows a wide range of other HR web sites to be accessed

http://www.hrvillage.com/ – An American site with a wide range of resources potentially accessible practical material available through it

http://www.hr-guide.com/ – An American site with a wide range of resources potentially accessible practical material available through it

http://www.acas.org.uk/ – Site of the Advisory, Conciliation and Arbitration Service

http://www.cipd.co.uk/default.cipd – Chartered Institute of Personnel and Development

http://www.dfes.gov.uk/ – Department for Children, Schools and Families

http://www.direct.gov.uk (wide range of information, some of which has HRM relevance)

http://www.dius.gov.uk – Department for Innovation, Unversities and Skills (DIUS) (wide range of information, some of which has HRM relevance)

http://www.berr-gov.uk – Department for Business Enterprise and Regulatory Reform (DBERR) http://www.employmenttribunals.gov.uk/ – Employment Tribunals website

http://www.employment-studies.co.uk/main/index.php – Institute for Employment Studies (IES)

http://www.equalityhumanrights.com – Equality and Human Rights Commission website (brings together a wide range of material associated with human rights in a work context)

http://www.investorsinpeople.co.uk/Pages/Home.aspx – Investors in People website

http://www.personneltoday.com/Home/Default.aspx – Personnel Today Magazine website

http://www.tuc.org.uk/ – Trades Union Congress website

http://www.theworkfoundation.com/index.aspx – The Work Foundation website

http://www.peoplemanagement.co.uk/pm – magazine from the CIPD

http://www.ilo.org/ – International Labour Organization (part of the UN)

http://www.hse.gov.uk/ – Health and Safety/Commission Health and Safety Executive website

index

Page numbers in *italics* refer to tables; those in **bold** indicate section headings; *g* denotes glossary definitions.

360 degree appraisal 62, 174*g*
absence control policy 125–6
ACAS (Advisory, Conciliation and
    Arbitration Service) 5, 34, 97, 174*g*
accidents and injuries
  compensation for 111
  HSE statistics 110–11
  liability for 114–15
action learning 49, 50, 174*g*
advertising posts 39
affinity benefits 76, 174*g*
affirmative action organisations 107
age of organisation 24
analytical job evaluation 71, 174*g*
anti-discrimination legislation 31–2,
    33–4, 100–1, 102, 103
appeals (disciplinary and grievance
    procedures) 96–7
  Employment Appeal Tribunals
    (EAT) 98
appointment of job applicants 40–1
  delayed 44, 178*g*
assessment centres 40, 174*g*
assignments *see* essay and exam
    questions
attitude 174*g*
  encouragement of employees' 85
autonomous work groups *see*
    self-managed teams

balanced business scorecard
    59, 126, 175*g*
Bartlett, C.A. and Goshal, S. 139
base pay 67, *68*, 175*g*
  determination of 70–2
Becker, B. et al. 126
Beer, M. et al. 15, 123–4

behaviourist learning models 47
Belbin, M. 105
benchmark job 175*g*
benefits *68*, *69*, 75–7, 175*g*
  physical welfare 117
  and remuneration **66–78**
  sick pay 32
best practice model of HR strategy 123
Boxall, P. and Purcell, J. 16
broadbanding 72, 175*g*
bullying 116, 176*g*
bureaucratic organisations 21, 176*g*
business
  competition levels in 19
  dominant view of people in 11
  nature of 11–12
  strategy and HR 121–2, 125–8

career progression 79, 176*g*
carer's rights 32
Central Arbitration Committee (CAC)
    83, 176*g*
club culture in relation to diversity 106
cognitive learning models 47
collective bargaining 73, 79, 176*g*
commitment 19, 23, 177*g*
  vs compliance 57–8
communication 177*g*
  business strategy and HR strategy 122
  cross-cultural 139–40
  downward 84
  knowledge facilitators 54
compensation
  for illness and injury 111
  for unfair dismissal 98
competency-based pay 71, 177*g*
competition levels in industry 19

competitive advantage 124, 177*g*
complaints 93
compliance 177*g*
   organisational approaches to equality
      and diversity 106
   vs commitment 57–8
compliance organisations 107
constructive dismissal 98, 177*g*
constructivist learning models 48–9
consultancy support for
      HR department 127
consultation 29–30, 82, 83, 84, 177*g*
contingency model of HR
      strategy 124
continuous improvement 50, 177*g*
contract of employment 26, 27–8
contract manufacturing, international
      HRM 133
contract of service 26, 178*g*
contract for services 26, 178*g*
control processes 21
Control of Substances Hazardous to
      Health (COSHH) Regulations
      (1988) 114
counselling 76, 117–18, 178*g*
cross-functional teams 64
culture 11
   and diversity 105–6, 107–8
   international HRM 132, 137–40
   see also organisational culture;
      social context
curriculum vitae (CV) 39, 178*g*

data protection rights 30–1, 178*g*
DDA *see* Disability
      Discrimination Act
decentralised support for HR
      department 127
delayed appointment 44, 178*g*
delegation of responsibility 92
delivery of performance 61
development
   employee 50, 179*g*
   organisational 106–7, 186*g*
   see also training
direct discrimination 101, 178*g*
Disability Discrimination
      Act (DDA) 31–2
disability rights 31–2

discipline 90–1
   and grievance 33, **90–100**
   in practice 91–2
   procedures 94–6, 97–8, 178*g*
discrimination 101, 178*g*
   anti-discrimination legislation
      31–2, 33–4, 100–1, 102, 103
   see also diversity
dismissal 95
   authority limits 96
   constructive 98
   fair 97
   unfair 97–8, 193*g*
dissatisfaction 93
distance learning 50, 178–9*g*
diversity 178*g*
   and culture 105–6, 107–8
   equal opportunities vs 101–2
   and equality **100–9**
   management 103–5
documentation for recruitment 39
dominant view of people in
      business 11
downward communication 84
duty of care, breaches of 114–15

e-HR 128
early retirement 44
emotional welfare of employees 116–17
employee assistance programmes
      (EAPs) 76, 117–18, 179*g*
employee characteristics 21
employee development 50, 179*g*
employee empowerment 84–5, 179*g*
employee expectations 42, 93–4
employee involvement 84–5, 179*g*
employee relations 78–80, 179*g*
   common law obligations *27*
   impact of legislation on 12
   negotiating in 87–8
   pay objectives 67
   policy and retention 43
   relative power balance 12
   and representation **78–89**
employee representation 80–3
   see also trade unions
employee rights *27*
employee surplus, management of 43–5
employee training *see* training

employee welfare 116–17
Employment Appeal Tribunals (EAT) 98
employment consultants 41
employment legislation 12,
    26–35, 179*g*
employment pattern 20
Employment Tribunals 26, 33–4,
    97–8, 180*g*
  see also hearings
enforced redundancy 44
enforcement of legislative rights 33–4
equal opportunities vs diversity 101–2
Equal Pay Act (1970) 29
equality 32–3, 180*g*
  approaches to 102–3
  and diversity **100–9**
  legislation 31–2, 33–4, 100–1, 102, 103
  organisational approaches 106–8
essay and exam questions
  interpretation **169–73**
    compare and contrast 172–3
    critical approach 171
    discuss vs critique 172
    evaluation 173
    missing the question 170
    parts analysis 171
    understanding the question 171–2
  subjects
    employee relations and
      representation 88–9
    equality and diversity 108–9
    grievance and discipline 98–9
    health, safety and welfare 119–20
    international HRM 140–1
    legal context 34–5
    organisations 24–5
    performance management 65–6
    planning, resourcing and retention
      45–6
    remuneration and benefit
      management 77–8
    social context 16–17
    strategy 130–1
    training and development 54–5
essay writing **150–6**
  adversarial system 151
  conclusion 156
  finding major questions 154
  getting into the flow 150
  introduction 155

essay writing *cont.*
  listing and linking key concepts 150–1
  outline structure 152–3
  rest your case 154
  stirring up passions 151–2
  tributary principle 150
  use of quotations 155
  'warm up' 150
exams **163–8**
  concentration 167
  coping with stress 163–4, 168
  'name dropping' 167–8
  practical details 166–7
  task management 166
  time management 164–6
  see also essay and exam questions;
    revision
exclusionary organisations 106
expatriation *see under* international
  HRM
expectations
  employee 42, 93–4
  employer 92 .
experiential learning models 48
export of goods and services 132–3
extrinsic rewards 69, 180*g*, 182*g*

factual complaints 93
family-friendly practices 42
'felt fair' systems 66, *67*, 68, 180*g*
financial assistance benefits 75, 180*g*
financial participation 84, 180*g*
First Aid Regulations (1981) 114
Fisher, R. and Ury, W. 87–8
fixed-term contracts 100, 181*g*
flexibility 15, 123, 181*g*
Fombrum, C.J. et al. 15
formal approaches to discipline 94–6
formal assessment and reward of
  performance 61
formal hearings, grievance procedures 96
franchising, international HRM 133
functional structure, international
  HRM 134
functional teams 64

geographical divisional structure,
  international HRM 134
go slows 86, 181*g*
grade structures 71

grievance 181*g*
  and discipline 33, **90–100**
  in practice 92–4
  procedures 96–7
gross misconduct 95, 181*g*
group influences 12
Guest, D. 123

harassment 116, 176*g*
Harvard model of HR strategy 123–4
Health and Safety at Work Act (1974)
    31, 113, 114
Health and Safety Commission 31, 112
Health and Safety (Consultation with
    Employees) Regulations (1996) 114
Health and Safety Executive (HSE) 110–
    11, 112–13, 114, 119
health, safety and welfare **110–21**
  business case for 111–12
  civil remedies 114–15
  employee assistance programmes
    (EAPs) 76, 117–18
  employee welfare 116–17
  legislative provision 31, 113–14
  occupational health departments 118
  risk management and assessment 119
  safety committees and
    representatives 115–16
  scope 110–11
hearings, disciplinary and grievance
    procedures 96
Hendry, C. et al. 15–16
high performance organisations
    60, 64, 181*g*
high performance teams 63
history of organisation 24
Hodgetts, R.M and Luthans, F. 139
Hofstede, G. 137–8
holding company structure,
    international HRM 134
holidays 76
home country nationals 135
Honey, P. and Mumford, A. 48
hopes and fears *see* expectations
HSE *see* Health and Safety Executive
human capital 124, 181–2*g*
human relations movement 5, 182*g*
human resource management (HRM)
  definitions 3–4, 181*g*
  emergence 5

human resource management
    (HRM) *cont.*
  'hard' and 'soft' versions 6–7
  origins 4–5
  specialisms and commonalities
    within 7–8
  underlying themes 11–13
  vs line management responsibility
    128–30
  vs personnel management 6–8
human resource planning *see* planning
humane bureaucracy origins of
    HRM 4–5

incentive schemes 64, *68*, 73–5, 182*g*
incremental pay progression 72, 182*g*
indirect discrimination 101, 182*g*
individuality 12, 137
induction 42, 91, 182*g*
industrial action 85–7, 182*g*
industrial restructuring 79
informal approaches to discipline 94
informal hearings, grievance
    procedures 96
information sharing 84
injuries *see* accidents and injuries
instrumental approach to work
    60, 182*g*
interlinked contexts model 15–16
international cadre 135
international divisional structure 134
international HRM **131–41**
  activities and approaches 132–4
  culture issues 132, 137–40
  expatriation 180*g*
    vs localisation 135–6
  global strategy, local action 131–2
intrinsic rewards 69, 182*g*
investigation, grievance
    procedures 95

Jackson, B.W. et al. 106–7
job classification 71, 183*g*
job description 38, 71, 183*g*
job design 22, 183*g*
  and retention 43
job evaluation 71, 183*g*
job family 70, 183*g*
job ranking 71
job role identification 61

Kaplan, R. and Norton, D. 126
Kazenbach, J.R. and Smith, D.K. 63
knowledge architects 54
knowledge aware people 54
knowledge facilitators 54
knowledge management
  53–4, 183*g*
Kolb learning model 48

labour markets 39, 183–4*g*
  see also planning
labour turnover 111, 126, 184*g*
LaFasto, F. 106
Lank, E. 53–4
learning 184*g*
  evaluation 51–2
  methods 50
  training and development 46–9
learning organisations 52–3, 184*g*
lectures **144–6**
  developing independent study 145
  development of 146
  mastering technical terms 144–5
  note taking 145–6
  use of notes 144
  see also seminars
Legge, K. 6–7
legislation 19–20
  anti-discrimination 31–2, 33–4,
    100–1, 102, 103
  anti-trade union 79
  employment 12, **26–35**, 179*g*
  health and safety 31, 113–14
licensing, international HRM 133
LIFO ('last in, first out') 44, 184*g*
line managers 43, 57, 184*g*
  vs HR responsibilities 128–30
location of organisation 23
lockouts 86, 184*g*

managed teams 64
management contracts, international
  HRM 133
Management of Health and Safety at
  Work Regulations (1992) 114
management preferences and
  intentions 22
management style 22
  and discipline 92
  and performance 58

management style *cont.*
  and retention 43
  and welfare 116
management teams 64
managerial discipline 92
market pricing 71, 184*g*
Martin, J. 12, 56, 57, 58, 87
masculinity, national and
  organisational culture 138
maternity rights 32
matrix organisations 184*g*
  international HRM 134
mental models 53
mentoring 50, 184*g*
midpoint, wage progression 72–3, 184*g*
minimum wage 29, 185*g*
monitoring learning 50
monitoring performance 57, 61
motivation 60, 185*g*
  see also total reward
multi-union recognition 82, 185*g*
multicultural organisations 107, 137
Mumford, A. 52
  Honey, P. and 48

national culture *see* culture; social
  context
negligence, liability for 114–15
negotiated consent origins of HRM 5
negotiation 185*g*
  in employee relations 87–8
'new pay' 69, 185*g*
non-analytical job evaluation 71, 185*g*
non-tangible rewards 69

objectives 185*g*
  clarity and scope of 59
  pay 67
  SMART 61, 191*g*
occupational health departments
  118, 185*g*
organisational culture 11, 23,
  137–8, 185*g*
  and decline of trade union
    membership 80
  and discipline 92
  and diversity 105–6, 107–8
organisational design and retention 43
organisational development
  106–7, 186*g*

organisational effectiveness, impact of learning on 51–2
organisational justice 90–1, 186*g*
organisational purpose and philosophy 20
organisational reputation 44, 111
organisational structure 21, 186*g*
organisations
  HRM in **18–25**
  origins of HRM 5
outsourcing HR services 126, 127–8, 186*g*
overtime restriction 86

paired comparisons 71, 186*g*
paternity rights 32
pay
  base 67, *68*, 70–2, 175*g*
  competency-based 71, 177*g*
  objectives 67
  sick 32
  skill-based pay 71, 191*g*
  spot rate 72, 191*g*
pay progression 72–3, 186*g*
pay reviews 73
pay surveys 71, 186*g*
peer appraisal 62, 186*g*
performance
  definitions 56–7, 186*g*
  impact of learning on 51
  see also productivity
performance appraisal 60–3, 187*g*
  process and perspectives 62–3
  stages 60–1
performance management **56–66**, 187*g*
  employee welfare 116
  issues 58–60
performance measures 59, 62
performance planning 61, 187*g*
performance progression 72–3
peripheral working 43, 187*g*
person specifications 38, 187*g*
personal mastery 53
personal needs benefits 76, 187*g*
personal security benefits 75, 187*g*
personnel management
  models 6
  'reformulation' factors 7
  vs human resource management (HRM) 6–8

physical welfare of employees 117
planning 36–8, 182*g*
  performance 61, 187*g*
  resourcing and retention **36–46**
  strategic reward 69–70
plussages *68*
points rating method 71, 188*g*
positive action 101, 103, 108, 188*g*
positive discrimination 101, 188*g*
potential team 63
power balance 12
power distance 137
premia *68*, 188*g*
principled negotiations 87–8, 188*g*
problem-solving teams 64
product structure, international HRM 134
product/service industry, nature of 16
product/service-related team activities 64
productivity 19, 188*g*
  bonus schemes 47, *68*
  see also performance
profitability 22–3
promotion 42, 188*g*
proprietary schemes 71
pseudo-team 63
psychological contract 28, 58–9, 189*g*
psychometric testing 40, 189*g*

quality circles 84, 189*g*

re-engagement following unfair dismissal 98
real team 63
recognition *see under* trade unions
recruitment 38–40, 189*g*
recruitment agencies 41, 189*g*
redefining organisations 107
redundancy 30, 189*g*
reinstatement following unfair dismissal 98
remuneration and benefits **66–78**
resource model 15, 124
resourcing 38–41, 189*g*
  and discipline 91
  planning and retention **36–46**
retention 41–3, 190*g*
  planning, resourcing and **36–46**
retirement, early 44

revision **156–63**
alternate between methods 161–2
beginning 157
mnemonics (memory aids) 160–1
organised records 158
with others 162–3
past papers 158–9
return journey 156–7
summary notes 157–8
reward
and performance 60
planning 69–70
and retention 42
schemes 67, *68*, 69, 71
total 60, 69, 77, 193*g*
risk management 119, 190*g*
Ross, R. and Schneider, R. 107–8

sabbaticals 44, 190*g*
safety committees and
representatives 115–16
Safety Representatives and
Safety Committees Regulations
(1977) 115–16
salary structure 71, 190*g*
sales agents, international HRM 133
Schein, E.H. 138
Schuler, R.S. and Jackson, S.E. 15
scope of operations 20
secondments 44, 135, 190*g*
selection for recruitment 40, 190*g*
initial sifting 39–40
self-discipline 92
self-managed teams 21, 64, 85, 190*g*
self-management 85
seminars **147–9**
complementing other learning
activities 147
creating right climate 147–8
opportunity to contribute to 148–9
strategies for benefiting from 149
useful features of 147
see also lectures
Senge, P. 52–3
service centres 128, 190*g*
shared vision building 53
shift premium *68*, 190*g*
short-time working 44, 190*g*
sick pay 32
single-table bargaining 82, 191*g*

single-union recognition 82, 191*g*
size of organisation 24
skill-based pay 71, 191*g*
SMART objectives 61, 191*g*
social context 11, **13–18**, 19–20,
137–8
see also culture
social justice origins of HRM 4
social learning models 47–8
socialisation 139, 191*g*
specialisms and commonalities
in HRM 7–8
spot rate pay 72, 191*g*
stakeholder 191*g*
stakeholder model 15
Storey, J. 7
strategic HRM 123–4, 191*g*
and HR strategy 122–3
strategic reward 192*g*
see also reward
strategy **121–31**
business and HR 121–2, 125–8
global 131–2
retention 42–3
strategy model 15
stress 116, 192*g*
in exams 163–4, 168
strikes 85–6, 192*g*
subjective reactions 93
suspension 95, 192*g*
systems thinking 53

tangible rewards 69, 192*g*
task autonomy of employees 84–5
Taylor, S. 85
team(s) 192*g*
composition 105
discipline 92
incentive schemes 75
leaders 50, 192*g*
learning 53
performance 63–4, 192*g*
roles 63, 192*g*
work 92, 193*g*
technical assistance agreements,
international HRM 133
technology 16–17
termination of employment 33
reasons for 42
see also dismissal

textbook guides
  employee relations and
      representation 89
  equality and diversity 109
  grievance and discipline 99
  health, safety and welfare 120–1
  international HRM 141
  legal context 35
  organisations 25
  performance management 66
  planning, resourcing and retention 46
  remuneration and benefit
      management 78
  social context 17–18
  strategy 131
  training and development 55
third country nationals 135
Torrington, D. et al. 4–5
Total Quality Management (TQM)
    85, 193g
total reward 60, 69, 77, 193g
trade unions 193g
  and consultation 29–30, 82, 83,
      84, 177g
  decline in membership 79–80
  derecognition of 82
  range of 82
  recognition of 81–3, 189g
    legal 29–30, 83–4
  representation
    in disciplinary and grievance
        procedures 96, 97, 98
    forms of 80–3
training 49–50
  and development 42, **46–55**, 193g
  and discipline 91
  physical welfare of employees 117
transport needs 76

uncertainty avoidance 137
unfair dismissal 97–8, 193g
upward problem solving 84

vacancy identification 38
values see culture; organisational
    culture
valuing employees
  management style 58
  organisational approaches
      to equality and diversity 106
  total reward concept 69
victimisation 101, 193g
voluntary redundancy
    44, 194g

wage bands 72, 194g
wage legislation 29
warnings, formal approaches to
    discipline 94–5
websites 198–9
welfare 116–17
de Wit, B. and Meyer, R.
    121–2
withdrawal of good will 87
work behaviour, impact of learning
    on 51
work organisation 22, 59
work-life balance 42, 194g
working conditions, routines and
    processes 116, 117
working group 63
working hours 29, 32
Working Time Directive 29,
    114, 194g
working to rule 86, 194g
written warnings, formal approaches
    to discipline 95

The Qualitative Research Kit

Edited by Uwe Flick

www.sagepub.co.uk